BRITAIN IN OLD PHOTOGRAPHS

THE BEST OF SHROPSHIRE

DAVID TRUMPER

The History Press

For my lovely granddaughter Alice,
who always makes me smile.

ABOUT THE AUTHOR

DAVID TRUMPER was born in Shrewsbury and grew up in the town. He taught at several schools in Shropshire before his retirement in 2000. He has always had an interest in local history and photography, and has collected over 20,000 views of Shrewsbury and Shropshire, dating from 1842 up until the present day. He has had twenty-two books published, as well as his work for local papers and magazines. David is well known in Shropshire's historical circles, leading talks and historical walks in the area throughout the year. He has been married to his wife Wendy for over forty years, and has a daughter and two grandchildren.

First published 2016

The History Press
The Mill, Brimscombe Port
Stroud, Gloucestershire, GL5 2QG
www.thehistorypress.co.uk

British Library Cataloguing in Publication Data.
A catalogue record for this book is available from the British Library.

ISBN 978 0 7509 6030 4

Typesetting and origination by The History Press

CONTENTS

INTRODUCTION

Shropshire is the largest inland county in England, covering an area of 1,346 sq. miles. It is sparsely populated with a population of under 500,000. To the west and north-west it is bordered by Wales, to the north by Cheshire, to the east Staffordshire, to the south-east Worcestershire, and with Herefordshire to the south.

The area was once controlled by the Cornovii Tribe whose capital could well have been the Iron Age fort on the summit of the Wrekin, one of Shropshire's most famous landmarks. During the Roman period the land was ruled from Viroconium, the fourth biggest settlement in Roman Britain. Although some parts of the site have been excavated, a great deal still remains hidden under farmland around the village of Wroxeter. After the Romans departed a large area in the west became part of the Kingdom of Powys until it was annexed by King Offa of Mercia in the eighth century and later became part of a new shire called Shropshire. After the Norman Conquest the county was given to Roger de Montgomery and many castles were built to stop Welsh incursions. For many years after Shropshire's western boarders had been settled, it was controlled by the Council of the Marches who had their headquarters in Ludlow and Shrewsbury.

The county is cut diagonally into almost two equal halves by the River Severn. To the north of the river is the Shropshire Plain that stretches through into Cheshire and is blessed with rich farmland. The main towns in the area are Oswestry, Ellesmere, Wem, Whitchurch, Market Drayton, Newport, Shifnal and Telford. Telford was conceived in the 1960s and built around the towns of the coalfields of East Shropshire. It became an independent unitary authority in 1998 but for ceremonial purposes is still part of the county. In the south of the town is Ironbridge, the birthplace of the Industrial Revolution. It sits in the Ironbridge Gorge which is now a UNESCO World Heritage Site. Around Ellesmere the landscape has been affected by glacial drifts, which formed the meres, Shropshire's own 'Lake District'. Close by is Whixall Moss, a fenland rich in plant and animal life, which was saved in 1981 as a nature reserve.

Shrewsbury is the County Town and lies almost in the centre of the county and straddles both sides of the River Severn. It is rich in history and has over 600 listed buildings, which includes a red sandstone castle and abbey, some beautiful timber-framed buildings and a number of fine Regency and Georgian town houses.

To the south of the Severn is the Shropshire Hill Country, an area of outstanding beauty. The landscape varies from undulating hills and pretty valleys to the flat heights of the Long Mynd, and the boulder-strewn peaks of the Stiperstones to the summit of the Clee Hills, the county's highest peaks standing over 1,800ft above sea level. The main towns in this area are Bridgnorth, Ludlow, Church Stretton, Cleobury Mortimer, Bishop's Castle, Craven Arms and Clun. Ludlow has been described as 'the finest small town in the whole of England', while Church Stretton is known locally as 'Little Switzerland'. Bridgnorth is the largest settlement in the area with its High Town and Low Town connected by a series of medieval steps and a Cliff Railway, while Clun in the sparsely populated south-west was described by poet A.E. Housman as one of 'the quietest places under the sun'.

Shropshire is also greatly enriched by its wide variety of habitations from isolated farmsteads to pretty little hamlets and villages. It abounds in myths, legends and local folklore. It is also the birthplace of Charles Darwin, the author of *The Origin of Species*, Abraham Darby who built the world's first iron bridge, Wilfred Owen, the First World War poet and William Penny Brooks, the founding father of the modern Olympic Games.

1

AROUND SHREWSBURY, THE COUNTY TOWN

Shoplatch, *c.* 1895. This is a lively view of Shoplatch looking towards Pride Hill on a busy market day. The Victorian Market Hall with its bands of coloured bricks dominates the left-hand side of the picture. The doorway under the columns is the entrance to the Corn Exchange, while just beyond the lamp is the sign for the Broadway Oyster Co. On the right are the shop signs for Pelican & Snelson, the tobacconists, the refreshment rooms of J. Goucher, and W. & H.E. Tanner, the wine and spirit merchants. The large five-storey building is Jones Brothers' Restaurant and Hotel. In a directory for 1896 we are informed that the premises had just been rebuilt and opened as a hotel with comfortable beds, bathrooms, lavatories, electric light and moderate terms. The restaurant sold hot dinners between 11.30 a.m. and 3.30 p.m. daily with chops and steaks at any time. The brothers were also agents for Melton Mowbray pies, Ward's Epping sausages, Malvern brawn, German sausage and Lipton's tea priced at 1*s*, 1*s* 4*d* and 1*s* 7*d* a lb. In Mardol Head is the sign of J. Kent the pawnbroker.

Market Street, *c.* 1950. This is a view looking towards Princess Street. The tall four-storey building behind the bus was the new extension to the Shirehall. It was officially opened in 1940 and was expected to provide office space through to the twenty-first century. A new Shirehall was opened in Abbey Foregate in 1965 and this building was demolished in 1971. The Midland Red bus has just left the station in the Square on its way up to Abbots Road in Monkmoor. Starting at the bottom the shops on the left are Little & Cooper, the boot and shoe specialists, Alberta Batsford, ladies' dress shop, Thomas Bullock and Davies & Sons, both gentlemen's tailors. Top left is the premises of Robinson the jeweller, whose sign urges passers-by to 'Stop Here For Hospital Spectacles'. On the right is the herbalist store belonging to Healthiway, then the entrance into Talbot Chambers; notice the talbots' heads and the bunches of grapes on either side of the doorframe. A talbot is a type of hound. The two shops above the entrance belong to E.F. Afford, the dry cleaner and dyer, and the other is a second branch of Little & Cooper. The Music Hall with its Ionic portico was opened in 1840 and contains part of Vaughan's Mansion.

The Square, *c.*1945. During the 1940s and early '50s the bus station was in the Square. Even with the decerased amount of traffic on the road the area was very cramped and unsatisfactory. The Market Hall was built by the Corporation in 1596. Beneath the arches the Corn Market was held and the room above was used by the Company of Drapers to sell their Welsh wool and flannel clothes.

High Street, *c.* 1955. It is difficult to imagine today that, until 1933 when the bypass was opened, High Street was part of the main A5 from London to Holyhead. Ireland's Mansion on the left was built between 1580 and 1590. It was such a large rambling building that it was known locally as Ireland's Folly. In 1965 it was decided to replace the timber frontage of Lloyds Bank with a concrete and glass façade. The replacement won a Civic Trust Award in 1968!

Wyle Cop, *c.* 1890. The large timber-framed building with its 120ft-long frontage is Mytton's Mansion, built in the fifteenth century for Thomas Mytton who was bailiff of Shrewsbury in 1487. He was the man who barred the gates of Shrewsbury to Henry Tudor and his army, vowing they would only enter the town over his dead body. In the cold light of day Thomas realised his mistake, and by lying on his back in front of the gates allowed Henry to enter the town by stepping over his body, and in so doing saved his oath. The sign on the side of the building advertises Blower and Jenks, who were ironmongers. At the beginning of the 1890s they had just been taken over by Shukers. The large chimney belongs to Dodwell's foundry on the corner of St Julian's Friars and Beeches Lane.

Clockwise from left: Castle Street, *c.* 1962. Marks & Spencer after modernisation in 1961. Shopping then was much more relaxed than it is today, with people parking their vehicles outside the stores they wished to visit. To the left of Marks we have the shops of G. Oliver, who sold shoes, and A.L. Salisbury, who were leather merchants. To the right of Marks is Frank Newton's store. It was known as the 'Big Hat' because of its shop sign, a large top hat the size of two men made out of a piece of zinc sheet left over from the tower of the old Market Hall in Shoplatch. The sign was taken as scrap during the Second World War.

Pride Hill, *c.* 1950. E.F. Afford, tailors and outfitters, are housed in the building on the right. At first glance the elaborate ornamental frontage looks like stucco but is in fact cast iron from Coalbrookdale. It was made for a Mr Biggs, a florist, and the designs depict his trade. They consist of flowers and fruit, with the head of Pan over each window. Next to Afford's is Lyon's Café and almost opposite is a similar establishment run by Mr Honeychurch, two of many such cafés where weary shoppers could take a well-earned rest.

Pride Hill, *c.* 1945. The Crown Hotel with its mock-Tudor frame is the focal point at the top of the road. It was built on the site of an old Georgian house at the beginning of the twentieth century. During the Second World War it was commandeered as an officer's club. To the left of the hotel on the corner of Castle Street is Barclays Bank, which was replaced in 1959. The small convertible car is parked outside Masters & Co., gentlemen's outfitters, which was later taken over by Weaver To Wearer. Gouldbourn's chemist shop is next door while further up the road is H. Samuel the jeweller and Shrewsbury Gas Light Showroom. Next door is F.W. Woolworth's Penny Bazaar and in the building that juts out slightly is the clothes shop belonging to John Overy. The large building at the top is Morris's premier store; this was opened in 1927 and is now occupied by W.H. Smith.

Castle Street, *c.* 1955. This street has always been a busy thoroughfare with lots of shops, and for nearly four centuries the Raven Hotel stood here. During the 1950s the hotel accommodated such stars as Laurel and Hardy, Winifred Atwell, Frankie Vaughan, Lonnie Donegan and Adam Faith, while they performed at the Granada. The hotel made way for the new Woolworth's store in the early 1960s. To the left of the hotel is Whitfields ladies' store, Frank Newton's gentlemen's outfitters and Marks & Spencer. To the right are the businesses of John Cleland, shoe and boot maker, Dorothy Perkins, ladies' clothes shop, and Melias the grocer's. Across the road is the sign for Wildings, which is advertising invitations, cake boxes and wedding gifts on its sign. At the top of the road on the left is the side elevation of Barclays Bank, which fitted the street scene much better than the stark new building they erected in 1959.

Shrewsbury Cattle Market, *c.* 1925. This is a busy market scene one Tuesday. The cattle pens are on the left and the houses on Smithfield Road are just above. The photographer is looking straight down the sheep pens to the bottom of Meadow Place. The large building with the telegraph pole in front of it is the Albert Hotel. Right up until the closure of this market in 1959, cattle and sheep were still being driven to market through the main streets of the town. It was always a busy market and in the twelve months up to 31 December 1933 a total of 213,842 animals were sold at the weekly auctions. At the special sheep sales held each September thousands of Shropshire ewes were sold annually into the Midlands to be crossed with a Down ram and other breeds. At these autumn sales buyers and vendors travelled from all over the country and the different railway companies ran special trains to transport the sheep.

Left: Longden Coleham, 23 January 1899. The flood at its peak reached a height of 17ft 6in above normal, some 2ft down on the 1869 flood but still enough to cover the road. The houses on the left are known as Terrace Buildings, with the Co-op at the bottom and the Royal Oak at the top. The inn was first recorded in 1883 and was still serving pints into the 1960s. In 1899 it belonged to Trouncer's Brewery at the top of the road. On the right there are three more public houses; the white building at the far end is the Cross Foxes, the far end of the low terrace is the Hen and Chickens, while the first house in the next row with the sign is the Three Tuns. The boys in the centre are standing outside the post office, run by Richard Edwards, while the barber shop belonged to Ernest Jones. William Edwards, who acquired the business from Frank Poultney in 1898, owned the bakery. The passageway between the barber's and the bakery was called Pipe Passage, taking its name from the shop to the right where Mr Taylor used to make his clay smoking pipes and sell tobacco. It became known as Fairford Place in about 1900.

Opposite: Frankwell, January 1899. A lady stands on the steps of the Sweep's House in Frankwell Quay, watching the river rise slowly up towards her front door. The buildings on the left are still standing today. The house behind the gas lamp is the Plough, which was first recorded in 1883. It was closed in 1906 after the police complained that there were nine other inns within a radius of 190yds and that the house was frequented by people from lodging houses and a very rough class of characters. Just beyond is the Anchor, which was recorded in 1780 and is still open today. The house that juts out at a right angle at the far end is the Model Lodging House, which advertised 'well aired beds' for 1*d* a night. Until 1890 it was a public house known as the White Horse, which gave its name to a passage leading into Mountfields. The passage in the centre leads through to St George's Buildings. With the large number of public houses in the area the rather fine-looking gentlemen's urinal on the left was aptly named the Frankwell Relief Centre.

Abbey Foregate, *c.* 1937. This view was taken from the top of the Abbey tower looking back towards the English Bridge. The cyclists are travelling towards town by the old road, while Telford's new road, which was put through the Abbey precincts, is on the left. Apart from the Abbey, Curton's garage and the cottages to the right are the oldest properties in the Foregate. They are cruck-framed with parts dating from 1408. The building surrounded by scaffolding is the new toilet block built on the site of Woodnorth's grocery shop. The frontage was constructed from timber rescued from the buildings demolished in Barker Street. To the left is Rowland's fruit shop and Halford's café. The white building with the large sign over the front elevation is the Bull Inn. Its most famous landlord was Edward Edwards, known to his friends and customers as Double Ned. At his housewarming party in 1843, a spacious pavilion was erected at the rear to accommodate 383 guests. Dinner commenced at 4 p.m. and they were treated to 'a sumptuous meal consisting of prime venison and every other dainty that could possibly be procured'.

Bayston Hill, *c.* 1910. Bayston Hill lies 2½ miles south of Shrewsbury on the Shrewsbury–Hereford road. On the left is the main village shop. The boys on the left are standing outside the home of Charlees Howells, a beer retailer. The site was redeveloped into the Three Fishes Inn.

Pontesbury, *c.* 1950. Pontesbury has always been one of the larger villages of the county but in the 1950s it grew into a dormitory settlement for the surrounding area. The council houses in the centre were some of the first to be built and they have been followed by a number of private housing estates. The large shop and bakery in the foreground belong to Edwin Bennett, who established his business in the village at the beginning of the twentieth century. The area has been redeveloped and a new housing estate built on the site, which is known as 'The Old Stores'. The car on the far right, by the timber-framed building, has stopped outside of the village garage. In 1937 there was only one garage in the village run by John Hughes. He was advertised as an automobile, electrical, motor and general engineer.

Montford Bridge, *c.* 1920. This view was taken for Richard Mansell's 'Princess' series of postcards. The van, probably carrying the photographer and his equipment, is parked on the left. The white building is the Wingfield Arms, named after a local family who lived nearby at Onslow Hall. In 1896 the inn belonged to Col. Wingfield and consisted of a kitchen, bar parlour, parlour, clubhouse, seven bedrooms, brew house and cellar. The landlord was J.B. Whitehorn. The name of the inn was later changed to the Old Swan.

Hadnall, *c.* 1930. The photographer is looking down the A49 towards Whitchurch. The car is parked outside the New Inn that was selling Bass Burton Ales on draught. According to the census of 1896 it was first licensed as a beer house. In 1896 it was owned by T. Cooper & Co., brewers from Burton-upon-Trent. The landlady was Annie Kate Kewell who kept the house clean and in good repair. In December 1877 the landlord was fined 5*s* and costs for selling beer during prohibited hours and in September 1883 11*s* 10*d* plus 9*s* 2*d* costs for permitting drunkenness.

Shawbury, *c.* 1930. The car stands outside the Elephant & Castle. It was erected as a hotel by Sir Walter Corbet in 1734 and was originally a three-storey building with eighteen guest rooms and stabling for eighteen horses. In 1896 the owner of the hotel was Sir Walter Corbet of Acton Reynald. The licensee was Selwyn Hawkins and the hotel was occupied by Harry Hawkins. It had eight rooms on the ground floor, ten on the first floor and was reported as clean and in good repair. The Hawkins family were also listed as licensees of the Elephant & Castle at Grinshill.

2

THE OLD TOWNS & VILLAGES OF TELFORD

The Market Square, Wellington, looking towards Church Street, *c.* 1950. The market moved to this site from the Green to the north of All Saints' church in 1244. It once included Bell Street, Duke Street and Crown Street, but these were eventually built over. On the left, with its grand entrance, is the Wrekin Hotel. In the last quarter of the nineteenth century Thomas Taylor, who also had a brewery in Wrekin Street, owned the Wrekin Hotel. In the twentieth century it became a commercial hotel, run by Mabel Chinock, and later a temperance hotel. The ground floor was gradually taken over by shops. Stead & Simpson sold shoes and were there from the start of the twentieth century. After the hotel closed the upper floors were converted into office space.

The Clifton Cinema, Bridge Street, Wellington, *c.* 1980. Two cinemas opened in 1911, the Picture Pavilion in Mill Road that closed in 1927 and the Rink Picture Palace on Tan Bank, which later changed its name to the Grand, but became a bingo hall in 1975. The Town Hall Cinema opened in 1920, but was closed by 1959. The Clifton was a purpose-built cinema, which opened in 1937 and was occasionally used for stage acts. It closed in 1983, much to the disappointment of the local people who organised a protest outside the cinema on 2 April. The protest was organised by the Wellington Chamber of Commerce and among the protestors were Wrekin MP Warren Hawksley, and future MP Bruce Grocott. Note the film and the flying saucer on the right.

The Market Square, Wellington, *c.* 1950. The photographer is looking towards Crown Street on the left and Duke Street on the right. Walter Davies's shop is probably the most photographed building in the town. He bought the business from John Owen at the beginning of the twentieth century and he was advertised as a tailor and a complete outfitter for gentlemen and juveniles. Note the large sign for Boots the Chemist over Mr Davies's shop and the car and cyclist on the left turning into New Street. Melias Ltd grocery shop on the corner of New Street is one of a large chain of stores. Lloyds, a local grocery store, is on the left next to Hilton's shoe shop.

New Street, Wellington, *c.* 1950. This photograph was taken looking towards the Market Square. William Bentley was landlord of the Duke of Wellington, on the right, from 1870 until 1905. He sported a 12-inch beard and kept a rack of Broseley pipes behind the bar for the use of his customers. The inn was demolished in the 1960s and Fine Fare supermarkets developed the site. On the left is Sidoli's café, which was once an inn known as the Shakespeare. Heath's van in the centre belonged to a local baker and confectioner in New Street, who also ran a popular dance hall above his shop.

Church Street, Wellington, *c.* 1920. The building on the left housed the post office, the printing firm of John Jones and a local newspaper called the *Wellington Journal & Shrewsbury News*. The paper was founded by Thomas Leake, whose family kept control of it until 1965 when it was bought by the *Shropshire Star*. At the time of its takeover, it had a circulation of about 48,000. In the early part of the twentieth century the post office was opened from 7 a.m. to 9 p.m. on weekdays and Saturdays, and on Sundays, Good Friday and Christmas Day from 8 a.m. to 10 a.m. for telegraph business only. The white building in the distance with the porch is the Charlton Arms Hotel.

The Square, Hadley, *c.* 1905. Mr Shutt, the pork butcher, advertised home-cured hams and bacon and fresh pies and sausages that were made daily. A Primitive Methodist church was erected on the corner of Gladstone Street and The Square in 1841 and was rebuilt on a grander scale in 1871. It closed in 1834 and was converted into a cinema called the Regal. It later became a garage selling tyres before it was demolished.

The Green, Oakengates, *c.* 1970. This is a view across the Green to Market Street, taken from under the railway bridge. On the left is the Coffee Palace, built in 1895. It acted as a temperance hall until 1913 and was also the centre for art and science classes until the Walker Technical College was opened in 1927. Classes took place on five nights a week, and on Saturdays courses for teachers and pupil-teachers were held. The council also used the Coffee Palace for a short time, and it was also used as an employment exchange and a register office. Duncan Ball's hardware shop is on the ground floor; he also owned the footwear shop to the left.

Market Street, Oakengates, *c.* 1930. At the beginning of the nineteenth century there was only a very small settlement here but with the arrival of the railway, which raised its profile and made it more accessible, a thriving town soon developed. By 1854 the main street boasted a full range of shops and other amenities, including a number of public houses. The second building on the left is the Oxford Hotel, which at this time was owned by Lichfield Brewery. Next door is the butcher's shop of Albert Spendlove Grateley and beyond that is Lloyds Bank and Baker's shoe shop.

Oakengates station and the Grosvenor Cinema, Market Street, *c.* 1930. In 1857 the Coalport branch railway, which later became part of the LNWR, was able to purchase the old Shropshire canal to build its line from Hadley Junction to Coalport. It was opened to freight in 1860 and for passengers a year later. This station closed to passengers in 1952 and for goods in 1964. Other stations on the line were at Malinslee and Madeley. The cinema was opened in 1923, and was built by casual labour, the men apparently having to provide their own tools. The cinema was always a popular rendezvous, and in 1932 seats were priced at *2d*, 3*d* and 6*d*. It closed in 1967 and was demolished in 1975 to make way for the new ring road.

The Market, Oakengates, 11 December 1981. A market was established in 1826. With the arrival of the railway the reputation of the market increased and it was rebuilt in 1869. Until the Second World War the Saturday night market was extremely popular, spilling out along the main street. One local was so taken with the occasion he penned this poem, 'Oh Oakengates, Oakengates, where everyone congregates,/ On Saturday night to wet your lips, smell the lovely fish and chips,/ Beef and mutton, pork and tripe, rabbits and cheese and dates,/ If you want the hub of the universe, go to Oakengates/ I'm fond of a bit of sucking pig, especially on Saturday night/ No matter how ill you feel, it's sure to put you right/ I've tasted pig in many a land, off lovely china plates/ But there's none can beat the good old pig, that comes from Oakengates.' Oakengates had an excellent reputation as a pig market.

St George's, *c.* 1920. This settlement was once known as Pains Lane but changed its name after a new church dedicated to St George was consecrated there. This is a view down Stafford Street, named after one of the aristocratic families who owned land in the area. On the left is the post office and printing shop run by the Edkins family from the mid nineteenth century until the 1920s, when the printing business was sold to Herbert Price. Just above is John Owen's motors and cycle shop, while the building on the right towards the top of the street is the Elephant & Castle. Another inn called the King's Arms stood close by and at this date in St George's, sixteen public houses and beer retailers were recorded in the area.

Woodhouse Crescent, Trench, *c.* 1930. After the First World War Oakengates Urban District Council brought to the attention of the Lilleshall Co. that many of their houses left a lot to be desired and recommended that they should either be demolished or appropriately modernised. The council also developed a number of housing estates between 1919 and 1922. At Woodhouse Crescent 185 houses were built, with other sites being developed at Freeston Avenue at Snedshill and at Walton Avenue in Wombridge.

The Market Hall, Dawley, *c.* 1900. Early in the nineteenth century the township of Dawley moved from around the old parish church to this area. The Market Hall was erected in 1867 and was built out of red brick with an ornamental frontage and vaults underneath. The frontage was once topped by a turret containing a bell and a clock presented by Lt Col William Kenyon Slaney, who in a guide for 1882 was described as Lord of the Manor. Down Chapel Street at the rear of the hall was a potato market.

High Street, Dawley, *c.* 1925. The Market Hall is on the left and the building straight ahead is the Elephant & Castle public house. On the left is Phillips Stores, who had shops in towns all around the county. They were listed as grocers and tea dealers. The men and boys are standing outside Horace Smith's barber's shop; he later moved his business to Burton Street. The shop with the large awning belonged to Benjamin Preece & Son, a shoemaker, who traded in the High Street for over a hundred years. The gas lamp at the top of the street was lit with gas from the works in Chapel Street, built in 1857 and belonging to the Dawley Gas Co. Ltd.

High Street, Dawley, 25 April 1967. This photograph records the chaos caused by roadworks when the High Street was dug up to remake the road. The *Shropshire Star* headline read, 'This is Dawley High Street Today – A Hole In The Road To Beat Them All'. The County Council had set a four-week target for completion. This photograph was taken two weeks into the work and shows they were already off schedule. We are looking up the street towards the Elephant & Castle. The building jutting out on the left is Bailey's butcher's shop.

King Street, Dawley, *c.* 1940. The Royal cinema was opened by Dr Woodhouse in 1937 with the film *Keep Your Seats Please*, starring George Formby. In the1940s seats cost 9*d* at the front, and as you moved away from the screen 1*s* and 1*s* 9*d*. The double courting couple seats at the back of the cinema cost 2*s* 3*d*. The Royal closed as a cinema in 1961 before being converted into a bingo hall and was demolished at the beginning of 2008. The photographer is looking towards the High Street with the people just crossing Meadow Road.

Dawley Bank, 27 October 1966. The families that lived in these cottages had been moved out almost a year before the demolition men moved in to reduce their homes to a pile of rubble. A number of the families were rehoused close by in smart new council flats in Powis Place. Many, however, still made a pilgrimage back to their old homes on washday to hang out their washing. One resident explained to the *Shropshire Star*, 'We are not supposed to hang out our washing outside the flats. There are special drying cabinets, which are quite adequate. But when there is a nice day quite a few of us go over and use the old lines at the cottages.' The open aspect gives a good view of the Baptist church, which itself fell victim to the demolition gangs in 2000. The cottages on the right remain; one is now used as Cecil Walker's grocery shop and post office.

The Round House, Horsehay, *c.* 1960. Until the middle of the eighteenth century Horsehay was a farmstead and a few scattered cottages. In 1754 Abraham Darby II rented some land and built a blast furnace, which was in operation the next year. By 1756 a brick works was up and running, and the Round House was erected as a pottery kiln in about 1790. It was later converted into a dwelling and was occupied almost until its demolition in about 1970. Modern amenities were poor in the cottages, and two of the residents, Mrs Davies and Mrs Hoofe who lived at the Round House, are seen here setting off to fetch water, as none was supplied to their homes.

Madeley High Street, *c.* 1938. The road to the left is Station Road and the shop on the corner once belonged to Jack Jones, who was killed one foggy morning in March 1936 when he was hit by a lorry while delivering papers on his bicycle. The shop was once an inn called the Royal Exchange. Before it was de-licenced the top floor was used as a clubroom, which contained a large pulpit, reputed to have been used by John Fletcher, the vicar of Madeley who was known as the 'Shropshire Saint'. The poster below the advert for Goodwin's Flour is advertising the films *Sinners in Paradise* and *Hey, Hey USA*, starring comedian Will Hay, at the Clifton Cinema in Wellington.

The Cenotaph, Madeley, *c.* 1935. The history of the town dates back to Saxon times. In the thirteenth century the manor belonged to Wenlock Abbey, who extended the town by clearing more woodland. The Cenotaph stood at this junction until 1970 when it was re-sited in Russell Square by the new shopping centre. It was always considered a traffic hazard, and on Armistice Day the parade would completely block the road for the duration of the service.

The Anstice Memorial Institute, Madeley, *c*. 1935. The hall was built in 1869 in memory of John Anstice, an ironmaster who had died two years earlier. It was designed by John Johnson of London in the Italianate style and cost around £3,000. It is reputed to be the first purpose-built workingmen's club in the world. Its accommodation included a lecture hall, that seated 750 people, a billiard room, a smoking room and a reading room and library that contained over 2,000 books. The hall was also used for a variety of social events that included dances and theatre. During the redevelopment of the 1960s a pedestrianized shopping complex was built around it but this has been replaced by a road that now allows traffic through the area.

Ironbridge, *c*. 1900. The town takes its name from the bridge that was erected in 1779 and caused the growth of the town, perched on the steep limestone cliff overlooking the Severn Gorge. St Luke's was consecrated in 1837, and to mark the occasion James Thompson of the Lightmoor Works presented the church with a silver communion service. The new church was able to accommodate 1,062 people, and from the beginning attracted large congregations. On Census Sunday in 1851 the morning service attracted 500 adults and eighty children and at Evensong the congregation was 700. The church was designed by Thomas Smith of Madeley.

High Street, Ironbridge, *c.* 1900. The bridge is just out of sight on the left. The buildings at the junction with Church Hill are the Municipal Buildings. On the right is the ironmonger's shop belonging to Frank Beddoes. The boys are looking with great interest into the window of James Simpson's music shop. At the top of the hill is the church of St Luke, erected in 1836.

The Market Place, Ironbridge, *c.* 1900. The Friday market was started in about 1800. The market hall, on the left, originally had an open, arcaded ground floor, with two upper storeys and an attic. The open ground floor had been filled in with shops by 1847. Mrs Bartlett of Marnwood House erected the red granite drinking fountain in 1862 in memory of her husband, the Revd Mr John Bartlett, the vicar of Buildwas from 1822 until 1861 and a man who took great interest in local affairs. When the Market Place was altered the memorial was moved and hidden above the Waterloo Street car park.

A coracle man, Ironbridge, *c*. 1945. The man in the boat may well be Eustace Rogers, whose family have made coracles in the gorge for several generations. These tiny craft have been made since Celtic times and were once very common on the river. They were often associated with poaching, and there were certainly a number of poachers in the Ironbridge area. Men with colourful names like Fussler Potts, Nacky Brathern and Bunkers Owen all practised the art. Speed and manoeuvrability made the coracle ideal for swift escape, and when capture seemed imminent a coracle and its contents could easily be sunk with heavy stones and retrieved at a more convenient time.

The Coalbrookdale Co. warehouse, Ironbridge, *c*. 1890. This building was designed in the Gothic style in about 1840. It was built out of red and yellow brick and has crenellated walls, buttresses, pointed arches and a variety of other detail that makes this building unique. It was only used as a riverside warehouse for a short time but has had other functions, including a mineral water works in the early twentieth century and a garage in the 1950s and '60s. In the summer of 1976 the Ironbridge Gorge Museum opened it as the Museum of the Severn.

The Ironworks, Coalbrookdale, *c.* 1930. The Revd Richard Walker described the area in 1801 as 'hemmed in by rocky banks, finely wooded, that would be exceedingly picturesque, were it not for the huge foundries, which volcano like, send up volumes of smoke into the air.' The company became famous around the world for its ornamental work, a reputation greatly enhanced by its display at the Great Exhibition of 1851, with such exhibits as 'The Boy and Swan Fountain'. The building with the clock tower, in the centre towards the top of the view, is the Great Warehouse. The clock is dated 1843 and was added five years after the warehouse was built. The Great Warehouse is now the Coalbrookdale Museum of Iron.

Coalport looking towards Ironbridge, *c.* 1900. Coalport is a planned town laid out by William Reynolds in about 1793. It was built to link the River Severn with the local canal system and was intended to become a major port, shipping out coal and other locally made items. Joshua Gilpin, an American Quaker who toured the area in 1796, recorded in his journal that 'above 40,000 tons annually' were sent down the Severn. On the left is part of the china works founded in 1796 and made famous by John Rose, who had learned his trade at the renowned Caughley Works. The buildings on the immediate left have been converted into cottages, while the building with the turret is now a youth hostel.

Jackfield, 29 December 1952. A lady hangs out her washing to dry on the banks of the Severn just two days before the New Year. This photograph is looking back up stream towards Ironbridge. In the background is the church of St Mary, built from a design by Sir Arthur Blomfield in 1863 after the old church had been undermined and declared unsafe. The new church, with its unusual octagonal tower and spire, was one of the first buildings erected out of red, yellow and blue brick. It's hard to imagine from this quiet scene that eight months before the village had suffered its worst ever landslide.

3

AROUND OSWESTRY, ELLESMERE & WEM

Bailey Head, Oswestry, *c.* 1935. The Bailey is the site of the town's open market and the name recalls the castle built by the Normans, the remains of which stand behind the Guildhall on the left. The Guildhall, with its highly ornamented front, was designed by H.A. Cheers of Twickenham and was built in 1893. It replaced an older hall erected in 1782 on the site of the Wool Hall. To the right is Powis Hall, built in the Georgian style in 1839. This building once housed the Corn Exchange and the Cheese and Butter Market. The children are playing round the Bailey Head Pump, which was installed in 1776.

The Cross, Oswestry, *c.* 1905. The photographer has his back to Church Street, with Willow Street to the left and Cross Street to the right. The building with the clock is Cross Market, which was built in 1842, enlarged in 1880 and 1900, and extensively remodelled in 1903 at a cost of £6,000. The clock was placed over the main entrance in 1854. It was the idea of Charles Sabine, a local solicitor who organised a public subscription to pay for it. A legend in Latin was inscribed on both sides of the clock, which loosely translated reads, 'Time and Money, Space and Weight, by one fixed standard calculate.' The store to the right was owned by Francis & Beckitt, who were listed as wholesale and retail grocers, and provision merchants and expert tea blenders. Next door is John Anderson's People's Boot Market.

The Cross, Oswestry, *c.* 1930. The photographer is looking down Cross Street to Llwyd's timber-framed mansion on the corner of Bailey Street and just beyond Glasgow House that was occupied by Bradley's drapery store. At this time, the People's Boot Market belonged to George and William Morton who had other outlets in the county. Arthur Meeson's confectionery shop is next door and just beyond is Melias Ltd, who were listed as provision merchants. The two ladies on the right are in conversation outside the Maypole Dairy, a national firm of grocers. The fine metal gas lamp at the centre of the roads was erected in 1862.

Opposite: The Cross and Willow Street, *c.* 1955. The left-hand side of the road has changed dramatically since this view was taken. The first building is part of the Midland Bank which is now part of the HSBC group. The next building, whose site is now incorporated into the bank, was occupied by Llewellin's optician and chemist shop. Phillips's Stores Ltd was one of the firm's many outlets around the county. They were tremendously proud of their own blended teas and in the 1950s they were listed in a local gazetteer as 'frozen food specialists, grocers, and provisions merchants.' To the right are Dale Bros, who occupied that site for many years. In the early days they were pawnbrokers and sold a wide variety of goods and household furnishings. The Fashion Centre, with its ornate frontage and clock, is the Cross entrance to the Market Hall.

The Cross and Church Street, *c.* 1950. The photographer is looking up Church Street towards the trees in Cae Glas Park. The group of people are outside the shop of R. & R. Hughes & Co., which was founded in about 1868. At the beginning of the twentieth century they were listed as 'General Drapers, Ladies' and Children's Outfitters, Gentlemen's Mercers and Tailors.' Just beyond, at 1 Church Street, are Richard Reeves' chemist shop and four doors further up is another chemist shop belonging to Boots. The building on the right belonged to the Midland Bank and was built in 1890. About half way down the street on the same side are the signs of the King's Head and the Vaults. For several years the King's Head was the home of World Cup hero Alan Ball, whose father was landlord and also manager of Oswestry Town FC.

Church Street, Oswestry, *c.* 1935. The photographer is looking up Church Street towards the Cross. The church of St Oswald is on the left, hidden behind the trees and railings. On the right is the Wynnstay, the town's premier hotel. It occupies a late Georgian building and possesses a handsome ballroom. Over the front door is a magnificent porch, supported by two pairs of Tuscan columns. It is thought to have been built for Sir Watkin William Wynn, a local baronet and landowner. Two doors along to the right is the Oak Inn, first recorded here in 1792.

Cae Glas Park, *c.* 1930. The ladies with the prams totally ignore the photographer but the children are fascinated. The park was laid out on the site of Cae Glas Mansion, which was demolished in about 1834. In 1908 the owner of the land, Charles Jones of Rossett, offered to sell it to the council provided it was used as a public park. The council agreed and bought the 8-acre site for £6,000. After being landscaped, the park was formally opened to the public on 23 June 1910.

Beatrice Street, Oswestry, *c.* 1925. The timber-framed building is the Fighting Cocks, an inn since the seventeenth century when it was known as the Lower White Horse Inn. In 1727 it was owned by Thomas Edwards, a mercer who lived in Cross Street and he is reputed to have changed the name to the Fighting Cocks. Just below is the sign of the Acme Fish Restaurant run by Victor Owen. The spire in the background belongs to the Wesleyan chapel, built in 1870 and demolished in 1964. The shop on the corner was occupied by Sarah Baker, a stationer, fancy goods dealer and sub-postmistress. The site was later occupied by Oswestry Industrial Co-operative Society. The garage selling Pratt's petrol and Mobil and Dragon motor oil belongs to Jabez Arthur, who had other garages on Smithfield Street and Oswald Road.

The Square, Gobowen, *c.* 1950. The car in the centre is just going over the level crossing. Note the crossing gates on the left and the signal above the trees. The little boy on the left is standing outside the Cross Foxes Hotel. In 1896 it was owned by Mrs Elizabeth Griffith of Gobowen and was first licensed at the end of the eighteenth century. The landlord was David Price, who was reputed to be a good manager, keeping the premises clean and tidy. In 1893, the landlord was taken to court on three counts for permitting drunkenness on the premises but all charges were dismissed. By 1901 the hotel was owned by Dorsett Owen & Co. of Oswestry. The lady on the right is outside Walter Benjamin Jones's newsagent, tobacconist and stationers shop.

Orthopaedic hospital, Gobowen, *c.* 1925. The foundations of this world-famous hospital were laid at Baschurch at the beginning of the twentieth century when Agnes Hunt and her friend Emily Goodford opened a convalescent home for the Salop Infirmary at Florence House in Baschurch. Many of the first patients were children, crippled by rickets and tubercular infection of the bones. Crippled herself as a young girl, she was forced in 1903 to seek help from Robert Jones, a leading surgeon, who performed a successful hip operation on her. He was greatly impressed by accounts of Agnes's work and, after visiting her at Baschurch, they formed a professional relationship that lasted until his death in 1933.

Whittington, *c.* 1920. This is a large village built on the old London to Holyhead road. The name is thought to be derived from the old English *Hwita*, a personal name, and means the settlement of Hwita's people. During the 1920s Whittington was fairly self-sufficient, with a wide variety of businesses that included a butcher, a baker, a maltster, a stonemason, two inns and a refreshment room. Edward Anwyl Jones, who was also a grocer, ran the post office at this time.

West Felton, *c.* 1913. The village lies 4 miles south-east of Oswestry on the old A5. It was built around an ancient motte-and-bailey castle that consisted of two mounds one on top of the other. The message on the reverse of this postcard is dated 14 March 1918. It reads, 'This is a view of West Felton the next village. The shop at the corner is where I go for my Woodbines and the shop just by the cart is where I get my necessaries such as writing paper. The post office here is where the extra-large telegraph pole is. The street to the right is where my boss lives.' Unfortunately, the writer gives no details of his identity or to whom he is sending the message to. The building on the left is an inn called the Punch Bowl.

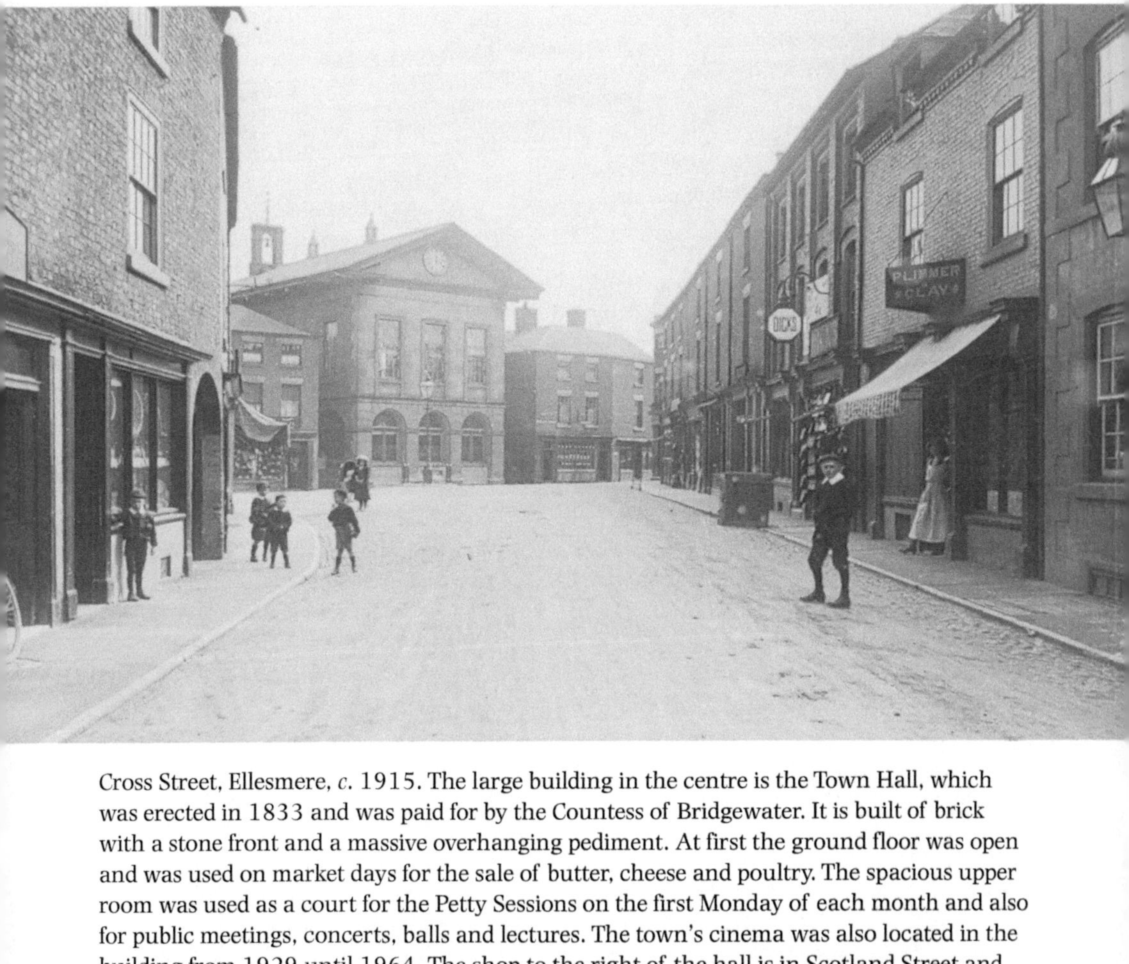

Cross Street, Ellesmere, *c.* 1915. The large building in the centre is the Town Hall, which was erected in 1833 and was paid for by the Countess of Bridgewater. It is built of brick with a stone front and a massive overhanging pediment. At first the ground floor was open and was used on market days for the sale of butter, cheese and poultry. The spacious upper room was used as a court for the Petty Sessions on the first Monday of each month and also for public meetings, concerts, balls and lectures. The town's cinema was also located in the building from 1929 until 1964. The shop to the right of the hall is in Scotland Street and was occupied by Thomas Povey, who was listed as a brewer. The bicycle on the left is parked outside the shop of Davies & Sons in Cross Street. They were tailors and had another branch in Market Street.

Opposite: Edgerley, *c.* 1920. This tiny hamlet sits on the banks of the River Severn between Melverley and Pentre. At this period the community was made up mostly of farmers but a boot and shoemaker, a beer retailer and a tax collector also lived there. The Royal Hill Inn in the background used to run a ferry across the river at this point. It was first licensed around 1800. Note the boats in front of the inn; the one on its side seems to be a substantial craft.

High Street, Ellesmere, *c.* 1905. This view is looking towards the junction of Scotland Street on the left and Market Street on the right. The building on the right is the Bridgewater Arms. The inn has a long history and was once housed in a timber-framed building and was known as the Royal Oak. It changed its name at the beginning of the nineteenth century, when it was partially rebuilt and was a posting house for coaches travelling to Liverpool from Shrewsbury, Cheltenham and Bristol. The ornate sign depicts the arms of the Bridgewater family. Across the road is another ornamental sign outside the ironmonger's shop belonging to Thomas Coffin. His son, Thomas Coffin Jr, had a similar establishment in Cross Street, which was also listed as a tobacconists, fishing tackle and cricketing goods warehouse.

Scotland Street, Ellesmere, 1920. Lloyds Bank has occupied this corner for well over a hundred years. Just beyond it is the Victoria Commercial Hotel, which was once known as the Bull & Dog. The building with the magnificent portico, with its Ionic pillars straddling the pavement, is the Black Lion Hotel. The large building at the top of the street is the post office. Behind the white building on the left is the square roof of the Savings Bank, which was purpose-built in 1830 at a cost of £360.

Opposite: The Square, Ellesmere, *c.* 1920. A large crowd gathers in the Square to watch the local hunt assemble. People are also watching from the upper floors of the buildings in Cross Street. The first shop on the left belonged to Reginald Sharp, who was a chemist and photographic specialist. The shop next door belonged to the Roberts family, who traded there for over a hundred years. In 1922, Frederick Roberts was listed as a stationer, machine-printer, newsagent, bookbinder and fancy goods salesman. The business was founded by Frederick's father Charles Roberts in 1872. The awning advertises the shop of Henry Welsford, a fancy draper, and beyond his premises are two shoe shops. The first is R.J. Dick Ltd, a national firm of boot and shoe makers, while the second belonged to a local lady, Mrs Elsie Pratt, and was known as the Boot & Shoe Stores. The building with the lamp over the front door is the Swan Hotel.

Church Street, Ellesmere, *c.* 1935. The road is named after the church of St Mary, whose tower can be seen over the roof of the Red Lion Hotel. In 1896, the hotel belonged to Earl Brownlow but was managed 'satisfactorily' by the landlord Thomas Jones. The hotel had twelve rooms downstairs, ten bedrooms upstairs and accommodation for forty horses at the rear. Before the railway reached Ellesmere in the 1860s, horse-drawn transport left the hotel daily to connect with trains at Chester and Wrexham. At the end of the street, on the right, is the rear of Ellesmere House. It was the home of Richard Christopher Tower, the agent of Lord Brownlow's Bridgewater Estates. A nice terrace of three-storey Georgian houses stands opposite.

Ellesmere, *c.* 1955. The Boathouse restaurant was the idea of Lord and Lady Brownlow, who wanted to improve the facilities around the beautiful mere and to put Ellesmere on the map as a tourist destination. The building was erected by the Bridgewater Estate and built out of Silverdale rustic brick in a herringbone pattern with timber work of cedar and a roof of Renardo tiles.

The Shropshire Union Canal, Ellesmere, *c.* 1910. The buildings at the junction are Beech House and the old Canal Arms. Beech House was built in 1806 as the canal office. It housed a committee room, a drawing office, accounts department and a place of work for the resident agent and engineer. Situated to the left of the buildings was a large engineering works. The Canal Arms was only a small hostelry with three rooms downstairs and four on the first floor. It was owned by Lord Brownlow and leased to a tenant. On 6 March 1871, the landlord was convicted of adulterating his ale with salt for which he was fined 6*d* plus costs. The Canal Arms closed in March 1901.

Northwood, *c.* 1914. Northwood is a tiny village that lies 2½ miles north of Ellesmere. In *Kelly's Directory* for 1913, all the residents are listed as farmers. The post office and village shop was run by J. Nichols, whose sign advertises him as a family grocer and general merchant, selling coal, corn, flour and oil. Note the X over the houses on the left. It was the home of Gertie who cheekily wrote this postcard to Miss Clinch of Cheltenham. She writes, 'This is our large village, the cross is our house. We shall call on Saturday and might come for tea. So tell Mr Gilbert to treat us to something nice. Love to all, Gertie.'

Welshampton, *c.* 1920. This small village lies on the main road just over 2 miles east of Ellesmere. As its name suggests it is close to the Welsh border and until quite modern times Welsh was the first language in the area. For such a small village it had good connections at this time with a number of lanes merging in the village, the Ellesmere canal running close by and a station on the Cambrian Railway just half a mile away. In the churchyard is the grave of Moshueshue, an African prince whose father was the King of Basutoland.

Lyneal, *c.* 1910. The village lies 3 miles south-east of Ellesmere. In the nineteenth century it was also known as Lyneal-Cum-Colmere, with the first part of the name being spelt Lineal. The children are standing outside the National School, which was built by Lord Brownlow in 1884 for 100 pupils. In 1913 the mistress was Mrs Alice Edgerton and the average daily attendance was seventy-two. Most of the inhabitants of the village were farmers, but there was a post office and shop, a coal merchant, a wheelwright, a thatcher and two blacksmiths.

Colemere, *c.* 1910. The small village of Colemere lies 2 miles south-east of Ellesmere, close to the south side of the mere. A legend tells of a church that stood close to the mere that was destroyed by an army of Puritans. The bell was rolled down the slope and into the mere, where it remained for many years until an attempt to recover it was made by several yokes of oxen attached to heavy chains. As the bell was dragged out of the water, one of the bystanders remarked, 'In spite of God and the devil we have done it.' Suddenly, all the chains snapped and the bell rolled back into the murky depths never to be seen again. However, when a strong wind blows over the mere the bell can be heard ringing. Boats kept at the picturesque boathouse could be hired for pleasure or fishing from the Bridgewater Estate. An upper room in the boathouse, with a fine view across the mere, could also be hired for picnics and tea parties.

Grove End, Wem, *c.* 1950. This view is looking up the High Street towards town, with the Horse & Jockey on the left and the tower of the parish church on the skyline. The Horse & Jockey was once known as the Pack Horse. By the end of the 1960s, the coachmen's cottages on the right had become very dilapidated and were threatened with demolition. Thankfully, the building was sensitively renovated and adapted into a single dwelling called Dial House. Just above is Grove End House, a lovely example of late-Georgian architecture, with two sets of bow windows. In the 1920s it was the home of John William Sr, a veterinary surgeon and inspector under the Diseases of Animals Acts for Wem District.

High Street, Wem, *c.* 1935. This view is looking towards Aston Street. The clothes shop on the right belongs to Bradley (Chester) Ltd who had other outlets in Shrewsbury, Oswestry, Ludlow, Bridgnorth, Market Drayton and Whitchurch. Next door, on the corner of Chapel Street, is the Corbett Arms, selling Wem Ales. On the other corner is the grocery shop belonging to Hunters (The Teamen) Ltd; part of the building at the rear was a dance hall known as Kynaston's Ballroom. Next door is Phillips Stores Ltd, who also had a number of outlets around the county. Note the delivery cart and the errand boys' bikes outside the two establishments. On the left is the Town Hall and further along with the large flag pole is the Castle Inn. At the end of the nineteenth century the Castle was owned by Henry Kynaston, who was listed as a brewer.

Clockwise from left: Mill Street, Wem, *c.* 1930. This view looking up towards the High Street was published by Frank Hiden, who owned a fancy repository. The gateway on the left, with the fine ornamental urns, is the entrance to the parish church. The two cyclists are just passing a building that was once an inn called the Buck's Head. The carved inn sign can be seen preserved in the side wall. The inn was later converted into a temperance hotel by Mrs Walford before being transformed into council offices in about 1933.

Aston Street, Wem, *c.* 1928. This view is looking out of town towards Aston Park. Part of Aston Street was once known as Maypole End. During the 1920s, two new churches were built in the area, the first was the Apostolic Church in 1922 and a new Methodist chapel in 1926. The new chapel, which stands opposite the Apostolic Church and the old cemetery, can be seen with its short tower and steeple shortly after it was built. The sign next to the gaslight indicates the way to the works of Arthur Simpson, who was listed in 1929 as a hot water and mechanical engineer.

Wem, 19 December 1920. The unveiling of the war memorial was performed by Brig.-Gen. H.C. Cholmondeley. The 14ft-high memorial in Portland stone was erected in the churchyard between the north-east door of the church and the Union Building on the right. When it was unveiled, it had the names of fifty-six local men who had fallen during the First World War inscribed upon its octagonal base. The memorial was dedicated by the Revd Hon. A. Parker. The hymn 'Peace, Perfect Peace' concluded the ceremony, after which a large number of floral tributes were placed on the memorial by family and friends of the dead. The Union Building was demolished in 1941, opening up a view from the High Street to the church.

Opposite: High Street, Wem, *c.* 1965. The High Street is the main shopping area of the town, offering a full range of shops, banks and other public and professional amenities. Dominating the scene is the tower of the church of St Peter and St Paul. Over the years Wem has reared or attracted many celebrities, including John Ireland the biographer of William Hogarth, William Hazlitt the essayist, John Ashley the portrait painter, William Betty the child actor, and Henry Eckford the sweet-pea expert who settled in the town around 1880.

Wem, *c.* 1930. The mill has stood on this site for over 800 years. Until the sixteenth century the mill belonged to the lord of the manor but was then leased and finally sold into private ownership. The present building is about 200 years old and is Grade II listed. In 1819, the owner of the mill, John Boughey, planned to introduce steam power, which caused a number of prominent townsmen to threaten him with a lawsuit as they felt the new machinery 'will not only be a public nuisance but a private injury to us as individuals.' The mill was modernised at the beginning of the twentieth century and sold around 2006, and has since been converted into one- and two-bedroom apartments.

Opposite: Soulton Road, Wem, 13 July 1905. Henry Eckford, on the right, with fellow sweet-pea enthusiast Atlee Burpee from the USA, pose for this photograph in Eckford's nursery. Eckford was born in Stenhouse in Midlothian in 1823 and was known around the world as the 'Sweet Pea King'. He gained experience by working on several large estates, including the Royal Park in Edinburgh, before moving to England. He became interested in the sweet pea while caring for Dr Sankey's garden in Gloucestershire. He came to Shropshire as head gardener at Boreatton Park before establishing his own nursery in Wem in 1888. By the time of his death in 1905, he had developed around 200 different varieties of sweet pea with colour and scents many previously thought impossible to achieve.

Tilley, *c.* 1905. The hamlet lies just a mile south-west of Wem. Its name is thought to mean an open patch in the wood and is derived from 'Telga', meaning a branch or bough of a tree and 'lee' a clearing. At the beginning of the twentieth century, the majority of residents were farmers but there was a blacksmith, a tailor, and a private school run by William Whiston at Tilley Lodge. There were two beer retailers with one also selling wine.

Edstaston, *c.* 1930. Quite a busy community lived here in the first half of the twentieth century. Most of the inhabitants were farmers and worked on the land, but there was a wheelwright, a joiner, an insurance agent and a market gardener. Miss Whitfield was the secretary of Edstaston Tennis Club and there was the Harp Inn at Quina Brook. The church is dedicated to St Mary and is Norman, consisting of a nave, chancel and south porch. The church has three beautiful doorways, two of which are thought to be original, but all three have Norman ironwork. The bellcote and bells date from the nineteenth century. George Bernard Shaw was once a regular visitor to the village.

4

AROUND WHITCHURCH, MARKET DRAYTON & NEWPORT

Whitchurch, *c.* 1900. This photograph, taken from the south-west, was one of many superb views taken of the town by Josiah Rowland Crosse who had a photographic studio and a fancy repository at 44 Watergate Street. In the centre is the tower of St Alkmund's Church and just to the left of the tower is the chimney of the corn mill. The mill stood on the bank of the canal near the Wharf and was marked as 'disused' on the 1901 Ordnance Survey Map. In Roman times the name of the settlement was Mediolanum. It was known as Westune by the Saxons, but its name was changed after the Normans built their new church there out of white Grinshill stone, first by the Latin Album Monasterium, then by the French name Blancminster, before being anglicised to White or Whitchurch.

High Street, Whitchurch, 1908. Two rival candidates, Francis Neilson for the Liberals and Beville Stanier for the Conservatives, campaign for votes in the May 1908 general election. The election was won by Stanier with a majority of 951 votes. He successfully defended the seat two years later against a different opponent. He lived for a number of years at Peplow Hall before moving to The Citadel at Weston-under-Redcastle, where he died in 1921 at the age of fifty-four. The timber-framed building on the right is Mr Stanier's Central Committee Room. The writing on the cars was scratched on to the negative by the photographer.

High Street, Whitchurch, 27 August 1974. A busy weekday scene in a busy market town. Note the style of clothes, the two-way traffic and the butcher on the left with his apron and straw hat. The building on the right with the arches is the Town Hall and Market; built in 1718, it was the town's third. An open market was held in the dry on the ground floor while the town's business was conducted on the first floor. On the left is the White Bear Inn, which was first recorded in about 1800. In a report the inn was described as badly situated for police supervision. At no. 12 is Owen's shoe shop, established in about 1935.

High Street, Whitchurch, *c.* 1925. A county policeman stands on point duty at the junction of High Street and the Bull Ring. The three rounded arches of the old Market Hall are to the right of the car. The ground floor was used as an open market while the upper floor was used as a Town Hall. By about 1877 the building was converted into a bank and the arches to the open ground floor were filled in. The bank later merged with Barclays. The purpose-built Midland Bank to the right occupies the site of Bradley's butcher's shop, which was demolished in 1926. The sign of the White Bear Inn can be seen above the policeman's head. It was first licensed in the late eighteenth century. In 1896 it belonged to William Yates & Co., which had a brewery in Manchester.

Watergate Street, Whitchurch, *c.* 1925. A troop of men and a Sentinel steam wagon belonging to Leslie Reeves, a haulage contractor, lead the carnival towards the High Street. On the left, almost opposite the Star Hotel, is Barrow Jones, a wine and spirit dealer who occupied those premises from about 1880 until the 1930s. Just beyond and flying the large Union flag is the shop occupied by Ernest Speed, a tobacconist and hairdresser. Behind the steam wagon is another public house, the Lord Hill, which belonged to the Shrewsbury and Wem Brewery. On the right is Dick's boot and shoe warehouse that was run by G. & W. Morton.

Station Road, Whitchurch, *c.* 1905. On the left is the new factory building belonging to Joyce Clocks that was built in 1904. James Joyce moved to Whitchurch from Ellesmere in 1790. He was the son of a clockmaker and he set up business in the old Crown Inn on the High Street. As the firm grew and exported clocks all over the world they expanded into this purpose-built factory. Note the writing on the wall 'Joyce Turret Clock Manufacturer'. They were responsible for supplying many of the double-sided clocks seen on railway stations, which bore the logo 'Joyce of Whitchurch'. In 1964 the factory was gutted by fire, but despite the damage, production of their world-famous clocks was not affected. The firm was taken over by John Smith & Sons of Derby in 1965.

Dodington, Whitchurch, *c.* 1920. Between 1891 and 1900 Haslam, Barron & Storey were advertised as coach builders in Dodington. They informed clients that they made all types of carriages, that repairs were promptly executed and that competitive estimates were given. By 1905 Barron and Storey had departed while Mr Haslam had opened a coach-building business in Bark Hill. Joseph Hopley had taken over the Dodington works and by 1917 the firm was advertised as 'Joseph Hopley & Son, coach and carriage builders, automobile engineers & agents'. During the 1920s the firm concentrated more on engineering and opened another branch on Bark Hill. The building next door with the fine portico is the Congregational Church, built in the Classical Greek style in 1846.

Grindley Brook, *c.* 1920. The bridge carries the A41 Whitchurch to Chester road over the Shropshire Union Canal as it makes its way into Cheshire. Three locks are needed here to take the boats down to the lower level. Some industry developed on the canal side, which included a boatyard, lime kilns and a steam corn mill. The building on the right is the gatehouse to the mill.

Broughall, *c.* 1905. The photographer has persuaded the men from the smithy, a postman and two genteel cyclists to pose for this rare view of the hamlet. It lies a mile north-east of Whitchurch on the road to Nantwich. The main landowners were Earl Brownlow and Mrs Nottingham. Between 1890 and 1905 all the commercial residents are listed in *Kelly's Directory* as farmers, except for Thomas Walker who was the blacksmith at Cross Barns.

Ightfield, *c.* 1905. The photographer has his back to Whitchurch. The turning on the right is to Market Drayton, while the road straight ahead leads to Burleydam. The second house on the left is the post office. In 1905 Mrs Hannah Rogers was sub-postmistress and mail was received via the Whitchurch sorting office. Postal orders were issued and paid there, but for money orders and telegrams, villagers would have to travel to Calverhall a mile away. The boys are standing outside a timber-framed farmhouse. A war memorial commemorating villagers who died in the First World War was later placed on the corner where the sign post is situated.

Calverhall, *c.* 1935. The large building on the right is the village hall that was a gift of the Heywood family in 1875. In front is a large bowling green, while the building on the left is the village post office and shop. In 1935 the sub-postmistress was Mrs Edith France, with letters arriving daily via the Whitchurch sorting office. The shelter on the left was erected in memory of John Pemberton Heywood in 1885. This card was sent by Monty of Cloverley Hall to Mrs Pidgion of Canterbury, who enquires, 'Are you getting a calendar for Australia?'

Tilstock, *c.* 1910. The village lies 2½ miles south of Whitchurch. In medieval times the village was known as Tildestok, derived from the old English meaning 'the farm belonging to Tidhild'. The inn is the Red Lion, which was first licensed in the early nineteenth century. In 1896 the inn belonged to Henry Kynaston of Wem Brewery but was run by Elizabeth Maddocks. There were three rooms downstairs and five rooms upstairs, able to accommodate six guests. The inn and stables were reported as being 'in good repair and clean,' but in a similar report in 1901 it was stated that, 'the house requires painting and whitewashing and the stables repairing.' On the reverse Jack informs his mother and father, 'This is where I had my first pint of beer in my life.'

Market Drayton, *c.* 1900. This market town in north Shropshire is largely unspoilt and still offers a full range of shops and services. The church of St Mary dates mainly from the fourteenth century but it was heavily restored by the Victorians. As a boy Robert Clive, who was born nearby, is said to have climbed the outside of the tower, a feat that would have taken great courage, a quality he would have needed in his later life in India. The watermill was one of nine around Market Drayton that used the waters of the Tern as a source of power. The mill has gone and its site is now occupied by an electrical sub-station.

Cheshire Street, Market Drayton, *c.* 1935. The building in the centre is the Butter Market, which was built in 1824 so that the sale of butter, cheese, eggs and poultry could take place under cover. The roof is supported on Tuscan columns and there is a belcote on top containing two fire bells. Above the front columns is the crest of the Corbet family. In the 1950s the market was described as ugly and an eyesore, with many locals wanting it demolished, but, luckily for the town, the council decided to retain it after a very close debate. On the left is the chemist shop that was owned by the Barnes family from the beginning of the twentieth century and in the distance, just to the left of the timber-framed building, is Morrey's garage in the High Street.

Cheshire Street, Market Drayton, *c.* 1935. The photographer has his back to the Butter Market and is looking towards the junction with Queen Street. The new post office is on the left next to the grocery shop belonging to the Silverdale Co-operative Society. The garage to the right belonged to Thomas Hockenhull who started there just after the First World War. The building with the fine dome is the Town Hall which was built in 1897. As well as offices it could seat 600 people and once housed the fire station, library, market hall and cinema. On the right is the sign for Sterling's boot and shoe shop, Thomas Billington's clothes shop, the Salopian Arcade and the cycle repair shop belonging to Beresford & Co., who also had a tobacconist shop two doors further down.

High Street, Market Drayton, *c.* 1935. The large ivy-covered building on the right is the Corbet Arms Hotel. It was named after one of north Shropshire's big land-owning families and was first licensed in the eighteenth century. Thomas Telford lodged there in 1832 when the canal was under construction. The shop to the right was occupied by John Lockett, a bookseller, stationer, newsagent and printer. The building with the lights is an ironmongers belonging to Gouldbourn & Son Ltd. The business was started by Frederick Gouldbourn in the 1880s and also encompassed a grocery shop.

Shropshire Street, Market Drayton, *c.* 1905. This view is looking towards the Shambles and the rear of the Meat Market. The picturesque timber-framed buildings were built soon after the great fire in 1651. The house with the railings and the name Sandbrook over the door was the premises of William Sandbrook, a wine and spirits merchant. In 1856 the house was occupied by Benjamin Bailey Sandbrook and the business was advertised as the Grape Wine and Spirit Vaults. The business continued well into the twentieth century until the house was converted into a public house called the Sandbrook Vaults. The building on the corner has been occupied by a butcher, a fruit merchant and a fishmonger before being converted into the National Westminster Bank in 1962.

Shropshire Street, Market Drayton, 1920. The large Georgian house between the timber-framed cottages is Poynton House. It was built in 1753 for George Warren, a member of the Warren family who lived at Warren Court, a property to the left of the cottages at the top. The Warrens were solicitors and lived there for over 150 years. During the 1820s sheep stealing was a major crime in the area and Charles Warren helped to apprehend one of the leading gangs, known as the Bravos. After the trial two of the gang were hanged and three were transported to Australia.

Market Drayton Swimming Pool, *c.* 1935. This view was taken for Richard Mansell and was part of his Princess series of postcards. Although unheated, the Olympic-size pool was very popular, attracting people from as far away as Stoke-on-Trent during their annual holiday known as Potters' Fortnight. The pool was opened in 1933 after Miss Onions donated £1,500 for the building of a public swimming baths. The complex later acquired a paddling pool and an ornamental fountain but was replaced with a heated modern indoor pool, which was opened in November 1995.

Woore, *c*. 1925. The building with the impressive doorway is the Swan Hotel, an old coaching inn. In 1896 it was owned by Thomas Henstock of Hanley, Staffordshire, and was managed by Anthony Ellwood. By 1901 it was owned and occupied by William Rhead. The house consisted of a bar and six rooms downstairs and fourteen upstairs with accommodation for twenty guests. There was also stabling for fourteen horses during the day and twenty-five overnight. In August 1899 the landlord was fined 40*s* and 27*s* costs for selling brandy to a drunken person. The house on the extreme left is the post office. The postmistress was Mrs Susan Simister and letters arrived in the village via Crewe.

Tern Hill, *c*. 1905. This view is looking towards Market Drayton, with two of the station staff standing on the tracks. The road bridge in the distance carried traffic over the line on the main A41 between Whitchurch and Newport. The station was the third on the line between Wellington and Market Drayton, before it carried on to Nantwich. The station closed to passengers on 9 September 1963 and to goods traffic on 10 August 1964. The main building with its ticket hall, ladies' waiting room and gentlemen's toilet are on the right. The stationmaster in 1905 was John Jordan, perhaps the man on the extreme right.

Goldstone, *c.* 1905. A group of villagers pose for the cameraman outside the Wharf Inn. The tavern was first listed at the beginning of the nineteenth century and in 1896 it was owned by Henry Belcher, who lived at Gnosall in Staffordshire. There were three rooms on each floor and accommodation for two lodgers. The stables were undergoing repairs and there was accommodation for ten horses during the day but only five at night. The landlord was Edward Hanmer who kept the house clean and in good repair. In 1901 Mr Hanmer was still landlord but the inn had been sold to Pearce's Brewery of Market Drayton. The inn's custom came from agricultural workers and people passing by road or canal.

Opposite: Lower Bar, Newport, *c.* 1915. This view is looking up Lower Bar towards the church and town centre. The canister belonging to Midgley's shop can be seen over the shop window on the right by the corner of Salter's Lane. The shop was famous for its large selection of cheeses. The garage just above the shop belonged to Richard Evans who was advertised as a motor repairer. On the left is the Swan Inn occupied by Henry Lodmore. The inn was owned by Lichfield City Brewery and had three rooms downstairs and six on the first floor. It was described in 1901 as needing 'renovating throughout' and that the stables needed lime-washing and new cratches and doors. Henry and his wife, Hannah, were tenants until about 1917 when Hannah became landlady of the Pheasant in Upper Bar.

Cheswardine, *c*. 1950. This is a general view of the village taken from the steps of St Swithun's Church. The building to the right is the Fox & Hounds, an inn with a history dating back to the seventeenth century. In 1896 the inn was owned and occupied by Thomas Jackson who kept the house clean and in good repair. There were five rooms downstairs and nine on the first floor with accommodation for eight lodgers. In 1885 Mr Jackson was taken to court for allowing drunkenness on his premises. He was fined £2 9*s* 6*d* plus 10*s* 6*d* costs and his licence endorsed. By 1901 the inn had been bought by John Joule's brewery from Stone in Staffordshire. The landlord was William Ellis and it was reported that the inn needed painting and whitewashing.

High Street, Newport, *c.* 1900. The site on which the town stands was in the manor of Edgmond. It was a planned town laid out by the Normans and it was granted a Borough Charter by Henry I. As the new town was close to many ponds and lakes used as fisheries, the arms of Newport contain three fish. The church, which lies on an island in the centre of town, is dedicated to St Nicholas, the patron saint of fishermen. The tower of the church dates from the fourteenth century but most of the main body of the church was built in Victorian times. The large building behind the church is the Wine or Vine Vaults, which was replaced by a nightclub. Pedestrians today need to keep to the pavement, as this is now a very busy junction.

Opposite: Stafford Street, Newport, 1960. This photograph shows the full extent of the Town Hall behind its High Street façade. The building on the other corner is the Barley Mow Hotel, which at this date hosted the town's Round Table Club. It was first licensed in about 1800 and was owned by Sir T.F. Boughey. In 1901 it had seven rooms downstairs and eleven upstairs and it could accommodate ten horses in the stables. In 1893 the landlord, Jabez Pitchford, was prosecuted for keeping an open house during closing hours but the case was dismissed.

The Market Hall, Newport, *c.* 1905. The hall stands on the corner of Stafford Street and was designed by the architect J. Cobb in 1860. It cost about £13,000 and was paid for by the Newport Markets Company. It had two assembly rooms capable of holding 500 and 250 people and provided space for the town's general markets, held on a Friday. In the 1950s Nikolaus Pevsner described the architecture as 'debased Italianate' and many residents thought it an eyesore and a monstrosity. However, thankfully it was preserved and completely renovated in 1964. On the opposite corner is the Barley Mow Hotel.

High Street, Newport, *c.* 1920. The photographer has his back to Upper Bar and is looking down the High Street towards the Market Hall. The shop on the left with its display of plants belonged to Thomas Blockley, a florist and fruiterer. His shop is at no. 1 High Street and he traded there from about 1910 to 1925. The building in the centre facing down the road is the National Provincial Bank, which was housed in that building before the end of the nineteenth century. In 1920 George Brampton was the manager. Immediately behind is the Trustees Savings Bank at no. 21. The sign by the gas lamp on the left belonged to the Old Bell Inn. The landlady at this time was Mrs Ellen Stanworth who took over the inn from her husband Daniel.

Upper Bar, Newport, *c.* 1930. This is a fine view of the Shakespeare Inn on the junction of Avenue Road. The road on the left is Wellington Road. In the census of 1896 it was reported that the inn was open before 1826. It was owned by a Shrewsbury brewer, George Jones Holt, and occupied by James Carrier Brown. The inn had four rooms downstairs and six on the first floor and was said to be in good order although the stables needed lime-washing. Five years later a similar report stated 'ceilings of passage, smoke-room and kitchen require lime-washing.' On 3 June 1890 the landlady, Mrs Elizabeth Williams, was fined £1 plus 6*s* costs for 'selling ale to a drunken man'.

Sambrook, *c.* 1910. The village lies just over 4 miles north-west of Newport. It was a thriving little village with several shops, a post office and a school. In November 1914 this postcard was sent by Fred to Eric Jones of Lewisham, London. He writes, 'On this card will be seen a view of our "Borough High Street." You will just distinguish the P.O. chimney on the extreme left. It is very cold here today. Something like it was in 1916 when I was at the "Palace".' The post office was run at this time by the Tomlinson family who were also tailors.

Edgmond, 1907. The school anniversary was held every year on Wake Monday. The people of the village have gathered to watch the children 'Clip the Church', an ancient custom where they all join hands to encircle the building. The custom had died out but was revived in 1867. While encircling the church, the clergy and congregation sing 'We Love The Place, O God'. The National School at Edgmond was erected in 1847 to accommodate 147 children.

Gnosall, 22 August 1906. Captive ascents costing 5*s* were one of the highlights of Shrewsbury Flower Show at the beginning of the nineteenth century. But on this occasion the passengers got more than they bargained for when the balloon called *Wulfruna* broke free of her mooring and sailed halfway across Shropshire. It landed safely at Knightley Eaves near Gnosall. An untethered balloon ride like this would usually cost passengers around 50*s*.

Lilleshall Hall, *c.* 1910. The hall lies 1½ miles from the village and was built in 1829 by Sir Jeffery Wyattville for the Duke of Sutherland. It was described in 1902 as, 'a spacious and elegant mansion of white freestone, in the Elizabethan style, and architecturally is a splendid example of "the stately homes of England." The house was erected mainly by the Duke's tenant workmen, and the oak, which forms so prominent a feature in the edifice, was all grown on the estate.' The main approach to the hall is by the Duke's Drive, an impressive approach along a 2-mile avenue of trees. The estate was sold in the 1920s and became a pleasure park. The slogan for the attraction was 'See Lilleshall and know the thrill of living'. During the Second World War it was occupied by children from Dr Barnardo's before being transformed into the National Sports Centre.

5

AROUND SHIFNAL & BROSELEY

Victoria Road, Shifnal, *c.* 1939. The photographer is looking towards the island at Fiveways. The building in the centre is the Trinity Wesleyan chapel, built in 1880 to replace an earlier church in Cheapside. There was also a Primitive Methodist chapel near the High Street and a Baptist chapel off the Shrewsbury Road. On the left is the Union Inn, which in 1901 was registered as an ale house with a seven-day licence. It had eleven rooms and stabling for thirteen horses. The census also reveals that the taproom ceiling required whitening and the stables needed lime washing. Most of the trade came from townspeople, agricultural workers and travellers. In September 1895 the landlord, James Mason, was taken to court charged with permitting drunkenness on his licensed premises. The case was dismissed.

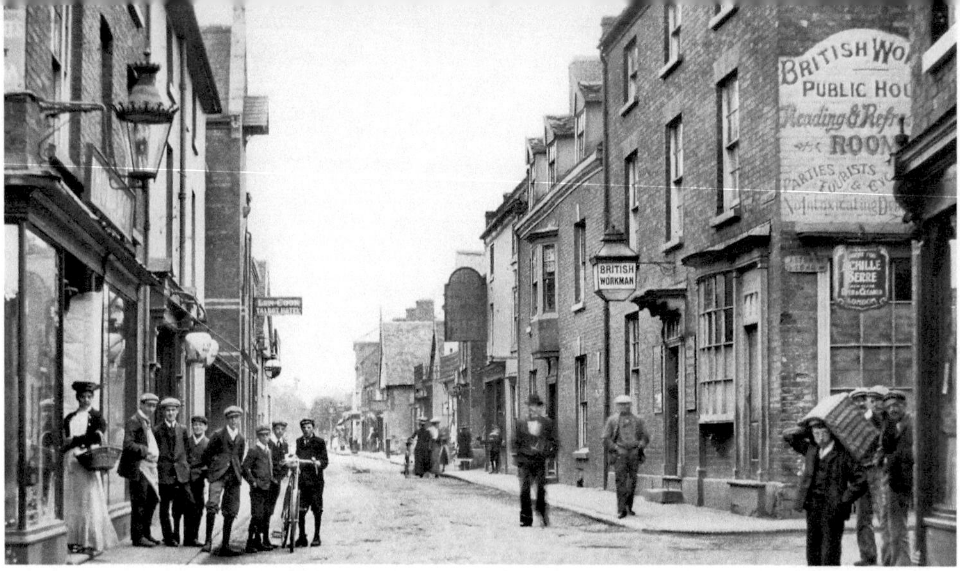

Bradford Street, Shifnal, *c*. 1910. This view is looking towards Broadway. The building on the left with the tower is the Market Hall, known to locals as the Town Hall. It was built out of red brick and contained a spacious room capable of holding 330 people for public meetings. Before the First World War it was used by the Territorial Army as a drill hall and it staged dances and concerts until the 1950s. The British Workman on the right was a temperance hotel and coffee tavern until about 1917. Before this it was a library and free reading room donated by Mr and Mrs H. Maclean of Aston Hall. Further along behind the gas lamp is the sign for the Talbot Inn.

The Beehive Inn, Curriers Lane, Shifnal, *c*. 1905. The inn stood on the corner of High Street to the left and Curriers Lane to the right. In the 1901 census the Beehive was owned by John Harrison, a builder in the Broadway, and was occupied by Richard Woodman. Accommodation consisted of four rooms downstairs, three upstairs and stables for two horses. It was reported that the ceilings in the house needed whitening and the stable limewashing. By 1905 John Harrison had taken over the running of the inn and it is probably him and his wife standing by the door. At this time he was listed as a builder and beer retailer. Another inn, the White Hart, is situated in the timber-framed house in the High Street and was there before the start of the nineteenth century.

The Market Place, Shifnal, *c.* 1910. The town is decorated with flags and the people are gathering for an unknown parade. Archibald Cureton opened his bakery and confectionery shop in the picturesque timber-framed building some time after 1905, taking over the premises occupied by George Woodroffe, a clothier. Burton & Nock, the auctioneers and valuers, traded in the building to the right and just before the bridge is the stationery shop belonging to Leonard Marshall. The shop through the bridge on the corner of Victoria Street and Cheapside belonged to printer and bookbinder Daniel Hall Jnr. Note the writing on the bridge advertising Shifnal station and the Great Western Railway.

The Market Square, Shifnal, 1960. The arrival of the railway in 1849 literally cut the town in half and the bridge over the Market Square dominates all the main streets of the town. The station was built in 1849 in an Italianate style using a pale yellow brick. The building was demolished in the 1960s.

Park Street, Shifnal, *c.* 1905. The timber-framed buildings on the left were demolished in about 1940. The inn sign indicates the Nag's Head. The business next door belonged to John Colyer, who was listed as an ironmonger, agricultural implement and cycle agent and china dealer. In the background is the handsome arched railway bridge that was cast by Horseley Ironworks in Tipton and erected in 1848 to connect the Shrewsbury–Birmingham line that was opened in November the following year.

Opposite above: Shifnal *c.* 1911. At the beginning of the twentieth century two events took place in the early summer. They were the crowning of the May Queen and Shifnal Club Day, which always took place on the last Saturday in June. The May Queen and her attendants were all local schoolgirls and after the crowning would take part in maypole dancing while the May Queen sat beneath the pole.

Opposite below: Shifnal *c.* 1911. This view was taken from the railway bridge as it crosses over Innage Road. Club Day was an event when all the local societies came together to parade around the town and to raise money to run the Cottage Hospital. The parade is heading towards the school and Church Street. On the left is part of St Andrew's graveyard, while the buildings on the right are part of Innage Farm.

CR
CR
CR

The High Street, Broseley, *c*. 1925. On the left is the Elephant & Castle, first recorded in about 1791. In 1838 the inn was owned by Lord Forester but by 1901 it had been sold to Stephen Hill, a grocer on the High Street, and was managed by George Millward. It was only a small inn consisting of three rooms upstairs and three on the ground floor. Another inn called the Albion is just four doors to the right. In 1901 the owner and landlady was Mrs Elizabeth Millward, perhaps some relation to George. The inn was slightly bigger than the Elephant & Castle with four rooms on each floor. It remained in the family until the middle of the 1920s, when the landlady was Miss Julia Millward.

The Lady Forester Memorial Hospital, Broseley, *c.* 1910. The hospital was built at the bottom of Church Street in a cottage style to fit in with its rural surroundings. It was opened on 8 April 1907 with twenty-four beds and a special ward for patients receiving radium treatment. During the 1930s R.H. Urwick was consulting physician, H. Macloud and W. Edmond consulting surgeons, F. Anderson ophthalmic surgeon, J. Boon medical officer, Lt-Col. Samuel Keyworth secretary and Miss A. Farrier matron. In 1941 the hospital had grown to thirty beds but by 1984 this had dropped to fifteen. The hospital became part of the National Health Service in 1948. To the right of the hospital is All Saints' Church. It was rebuilt in the Perpendicular style in 1845 at a cost of around £9,000. Since this view was taken the pinnacles to the tower have been removed.

Opposite: The Memorial Garden, Broseley, *c.* 1950. The war memorial was erected after the First World War in memory of the men from Broseley who had sacrificed their lives during the conflict. The dedication reads, 'Greater love hath no man than this that a man lay down his life for his friends. To the Glory of God and in grateful memory of the fifty-two men of this parish who gave their lives for King and Country during the Great War. 1914–1918.' The memorial was adapted to include the names of the nineteen men who died during the Second World War and Pte W.J. Boden and to Staff Cpl R.J. Bright who died in later hostilities. The large building to the right of the telephone box was built in 1900 by Richard Alfred Instone and was known as the Stores.

High Street, Broseley, *c.* 1906. The message on the back of this postcard reads: 'Broseley, Sunday, September 9th 1906. Broseley Friendly Society's parade in aid of the hospitals. This is the Madeley Town Band. Four stayed to tea at New Inn.' The large Gothic monument on the left is the memorial to George Pritchard, who died in 1861. He was a local solicitor and banker and a great benefactor to the town. Behind the monument is the Pritchard Memorial Green and beyond that Victoria Hall, which was erected in 1867.

Opposite: Tong Castle, *c.* 1900. The first castle on this site was erected in 1127. It was added to and rebuilt several times over the years until this structure was erected in the 1760s by George Durant. It was designed in a Gothic- Moorish style by Lancelot 'Capability' Brown who also landscaped the grounds. The house was occupied until 1908 and it is believed that Charles Dickens' grandmother worked at the castle. Part of the building was demolished during the First World War and was reduced to a pile of rubble in 1954 by a group of TA sappers who blew it up using 120lb of army explosives. Most of the foundations that remained were destroyed when the M54 motorway was built through the site in the 1970s.

Tong, *c.*1900. The name of the village is derived from the old English word *Tang* meaning a fork, referring to a fork created by two streams joining together close to the settlement. The village is associated with the Victorian author Charles Dickens who wrote about it in *The Old Curiosity Shop*. The grave of the fictitious Little Nell can be found in the churchyard. It was the idea of a former verger who even forged her burial in the church register, after realising that showing such items to visitors could be a profitable sideline.

The High Street, Albrighton, *c*. 1950. This junction with Cross Road on the left and Station Road on the right is considered to be the centre of this large village. Standing on the corner of High Street and Station Road is the Crown Hotel. It was first licensed in the late eighteenth century and was an ale house open seven days a week. In 1901 the condition of the house was reported as fair but the stables needed cleaning and lime-washing and the floor and ceiling repairing. The white building just behind the cyclists is another inn called the Bush or the Old Bush. At the beginning of the twentieth century the inn was owned by Ruben Blackham of Oaken in Staffordshire but occupied by Arthur Bowers. Like the Crown the condition of the main building was fair but the stables needed attention.

6

AROUND BRIDGNORTH, MUCH WENLOCK & CLEOBURY MORTIMER

Bridge Street, Bridgnorth, *c.* 1920. The bridge over the River Severn was built in 1824 to replace a medieval bridge erected at the very beginning of the twelfth century; it was partially rebuilt and widened in about 1960. The tall building to the left of the bridge is the Castle Hill Railway and Lift Vaults. On the right of the bridge is Ridley's Warehouse, established in 1616 and still functioning today. Bishop Percy's House is the timber-framed building in the centre of the view and in the top right-hand corner is the tower of the church of St Leonard.

Bridge Street, Bridgnorth, *c.* 1920. This postcard was published by Mrs Alice Ball who in 1922 ran a stationers and newsagents at 5 Bridge Street, which is the small house with the dormer window just beyond the lady with the pram. The taller building to the left is the Black Horse, which was occupied by Arthur Oliver at this time. The shop next door is listed as hardware and general stores. They have bicycle tyres on display and signs on the wall advertising Colman's starch and mustard, Milkmaid's milk and Sunlight soap. The car hire and accessory shop next door was part of John Ford's motor garage. The first building in St John's Street is the Falcon Hotel.

The River Severn, Bridgnorth, *c.* 1920. This view is looking across the river, downstream to the bridge. In the centre of the photograph are Bank Steps leading to the Cartway. Most of the buildings between the steps and the bridge have been demolished and the site is now used as a car park. On the far bank are the landing stages and pleasure boats belonging to William Corfield who lived in the cottages on the far right. The business started in the 1880s when William Corfield Senior and William Corfield Junior were both listed as pleasure boat owners. The business continued through several generations to the middle of the twentieth century. Their main competitor was Darley's Boats on the opposite bank of the river: that business was founded by Alfred Darley a few years after Corfield's. Note their large pleasure boat called the *City of Venice*, moored between their pontoons.

Mill Street, Bridgnorth, *c.* 1900. The photographer has his back to Bridge Street and is looking down to Cann Hall, which is just to the right of the horses. It was built on the site of an older hall in 1594 and it is thought that Prince Rupert of the Rhine lodged there in 1642 while fighting on the side of Charles I during the Civil War. It was later used as a factory making sulphuric acid and by a monumental stonemason. In 1958, shortly before it was demolished, it was described as having a 'Jacobean façade' and 'a good staircase'. There are two inns on the left. The first in the cottage to the left of the man with the wheelbarrow is the Crown and Anchor, which brewed its own beer. The tall building at the bottom of the road is the Bandon Arms, a large house with five rooms downstairs, eight on the first floor and stabling at the rear for twenty horses.

The Cliff Railway and the Castle Walk, Bridgnorth, *c.* 1930. The walk was laid out along the steep ridge between the castle and the Cartway and provides a superb panoramic view of the surrounding countryside. During his visit to the town in 1642 King Charles I thought that it was the finest view in his kingdom and is believed to have planted a mulberry tree in a garden there. The stations at the top and bottom of the railway were constructed by Bradney & Co. of Albrighton, Wolverhampton and Shifnal. The building to the right of the station with the rounded windows is the rear of the Wesleyan Methodist chapel that faces the Cartway. It was designed by Thomas Powell and built in 1853.

The High Street, Bridgnorth, *c.* 1950. The photographer is looking towards the junction of East and West Castle Street and the site of the old Postern Gate. The tower of St Mary's Church is to the right of Collins' shop with the tower of the new Market Hall to the right of that. The white building just below the church tower is the Shakespeare Hotel. The building in the centre was called Barbican House and it was occupied on the right by Collins' shoe shop and by Amos Ryder, who ran a draper's shop on the ground floor and a toy bazaar in the basement. The Swan Hotel on the left has been giving shelter to travellers for many years. In 1900 it was owned by Mitchell & Butler of Birmingham and had twenty rooms, which included a billiard room and an assembly room. To the left of the Swan is a fruit and fishmonger's shop which belonged to S.S. Crane.

High Street, Bridgnorth, 1935. The Town Hall was erected after the Civil War in 1652 and was built on sandstone arches. The upper storey's timbers are said to come from an old barn in Much Wenlock. To the left of the arch is a drinking fountain. The timber-framed houses on the right date from the middle of the seventeenth century. They stand on a site once occupied by a much older building that belonged to a family whose crest was a swan. In 1492 the building was recorded as Hospice Le Swanne. The Swan was first listed as an inn in about 1690.

High Street, Bridgnorth, *c.* 1935. The first shop on the left belonged to Little and Cooper, the shoe and boot specialists, who had a number of outlets in Shropshire. Next door is the Midland Bank and just beyond is the Crown Hotel with its smart canopy over the pavement. Beyond that on the corner of Whitburn Street is Lloyd's Bank. On the right the people are standing outside the Castle Stores, an ironmonger's run by Sydney Greatwich, who started off as a shopkeeper in Westgate Cottage in the early 1920s. By 1929 he had opened a hardware shop in West Castle Street before moving to these premises by 1934. The Bridgnorth Garage was opened in a building that was known as the Borough Stores Café and Restaurant until it was gutted by fire in the early part of the last century.

North Gate, *c.* 1950. The street takes its name from the gateway, the last survivor of the five medieval entrances into the town. Very little of the original structure survives as it was heavily restored in 1910. The small gate to the left was only opened to the other side during the renovations of 1910; before that it led to a gentlemen's convenience. The small window on the right of the tower belongs to a small lock-up known as the Thieves Hole. The Bear Inn was first recorded from the early nineteenth century; it used to brew its own beer and for a short while was called the Reindeer Inn.

Alveley, *c.* 1935. The village stands in the south-east corner of Shropshire midway between Bridgnorth and Kidderminster and close to the banks of the River Severn. The old settlement dates back to Saxon times and the village has a number of old buildings. This tranquil scene was taken at about the time that the Highley Mining Company sank their first shaft on the Alveley side of the river, an event that would alter the character of the village considerably. At this period the village had four grocery shops, a butcher, a post office, three public houses and two beer retailers. Two of the public houses had very old licences. The Three Horseshoes is reputed to have been serving beer since 1406 and is one of the oldest public houses in Shropshire, while the Bell Inn has had a licence since 1647.

Worfield, *c*. 1925. The village lies just over 3 miles north-east of Bridgnorth, close to the A545 to Wolverhampton. It is a charming little village which takes its name from the River Worfe that runs close by. The main road in the village leads to the sandstone church dedicated to St Peter. The dominant feature of the church is the sandstone tower topped by an elegant grey stone spire, which rises to a height of 200ft. The cyclists have just passed Clarke's Store on the left. The Clarke family ran this store from about 1905 when it was listed as a bakery and post office run by Mrs Charlotte Clarke and Miss Kate Clarke, the sub-postmistress. By 1922 Albert Clarke was managing the store and was listed as a grocer, baker and assistant overseer. The post office side of the business was still in the hands of Kate Clarke.

Opposite: The vicarage and school, Claverley, *c*. 1905. The vicarage is the timber-framed building that stands by the Lychgate to the side of the church and was erected in the fifteenth century. The vicarage was occupied at this time by the Revd T.W. Harvey and the living was worth £164 a year including 6 acres of glebe land. It was in the gift of John Beedham whose relative M.J. Beedham had been vicar of Claverley from 1867 to 1900. The church is dedicated to All Saints. In the nave are some fine medieval wall paintings uncovered in 1902. The huntsmen could be part of the Wheatland Hunt.

Clockwise from above left: The Cross Roads, Much Wenlock, *c.* 1930. The photographer has his back to the road leading to the Craven Arms and is looking across to Smithfield Road. The road in the foreground is the main Shrewsbury to Bridgnorth road. The house to the left of the timber-framed building was the home of David Henry Somerset Cranage while he was curate of Much Wenlock between 1898 and 1902. He had been curate of Little Wenlock between 1897 and 1898 and later became Dean of Norwich in 1928. He was greatly interested in local history and he was made vice-president of both the Shropshire Archaeological Society in 1929 and the Society of Antiquities in 1930. He was also the author of *An Architectural Account of the Churches of Shropshire*, which is still being used by a new generation of local historians. The single-storey cottage with the massive chimney-stack in Smithfield Road is the Squatters Cottage. To gain squatters' rights a house had to be built between the hours of sunrise and sunset on the same day.

The High Street, Much Wenlock, *c.* 1930. The first building on the right is occupied by Ernest Llewellyn Duckett, a baker and confectioner who also had a shop in Sheinton Street. The Talbot Inn next door is housed in a timber-framed building encased in plaster. It dates from the second half of the fifteenth century and is thought to occupy the site of the almonry belonging to Wenlock Priory. The inn was first licensed in about 1826 and it was once known as the Cheshire Cheese. In 1901 the inn belonged to J. Joule & Sons Ltd of Stone in Staffordshire. The shoe shop just beyond was owned by Tom Prestwood and was known as the Boot & Shoe Warehouse.

The High Street, Much Wenlock, c. 1935. The timber-framed building at the top of the street is Barclay's Bank. Parts of the building date back to the early fifteenth century and it was once an inn called the Raven. In the 1960s the manager Mr Hope announced, 'The fabric of our branch is old and charming like the town it serves. But the services you'll find here are as up-to-date as any customer of a modern bank has a right to expect.' The Midland Bank is the first building on the right. Opposite is the sign of the George and Dragon, an inn since the eighteenth century. In 1901 the George was owned by Charles Gaskell whose address was The Abbey, Much Wenlock. The landlord was Frederick Yates, who was also listed as a farmer. At this time the inn was reported to be in a 'Bad state of repair; roof bad, requires plastering, whitewashing, painting & co. throughout'.

The Guildhall, Much Wenlock, *c.* 1935. The Guildhall stands close to the Square at the junction of the High Street, Wilmore Street and Barrow Street. It was built in 1577 by local carpenter Richard Dawley. Borough records inform us that 'Upon 23rd and 24th days of this month of September was reared the house over the Prison House.' The prison was the stone structure at the far end of the building. It took only two days to construct as Richard Dawley would have built the timber frame at his yard and then reconstructed it on site. The area beneath the building was used as a market while the upper storey was used as a courthouse and council chamber. On the second post from the right can be seen the manacles used to restrain criminals while they were being flogged. The drinking fountain and clock tower on the right was erected by Thomas Cooke in 1897 to celebrate Queen Victoria's Diamond Jubilee.

Sheinton Street, Much Wenlock, *c.* 1920. The photographer is looking towards the Guildhall, the timber-framed building beyond the church. The smaller timber-framed house in the centre is on the corner of the Bull Ring. The church is dedicated to the Holy Trinity and was built in about 1120. The massive tower that masks the original west end was erected in about 1190 and the spire was added later. Unfortunately, by the twentieth century the weight of the lead on the spire was causing problems at its base and also with the foundations of the tower so it was removed on the grounds of safety in 1931. Note the large blue light of the county police station on the left. In 1922 it was manned by Sergeant Lovatt and three constables.

The Priory Ruins, Much Wenlock, *c.* 1920. The priory is the only religious house in Shropshire established before the Norman Conquest. It was founded in about AD 680 as a nunnery ruled by St Milburge, a member of the Mercian royal family who dedicated her life to Christ and to whom many miracles are attributed. After the Norman Conquest Roger Montgomery, the 1st Earl of Shrewsbury, enhanced the status of the priory, which over the years grew in wealth. The religious community was dissolved on 26 January 1540 during the reign of Henry VIII. Three churches are thought to have been built on the site, the last erected mainly in the early thirteenth century. These remains lie to the south-west of the nave near the west door. Note the tower and spire of Holy Trinity church in the background.

Church Street, Cleobury Mortimer, *c.* 1935. Cleobury Mortimer is a pretty little market town that lies 11 miles east of Ludlow on the main road to Bewdley. The photographer has his back to Lower Street and is looking towards Church Street with the Hurst leading to Ron Hill Lane on the right. Dominating the scene is the church of St Mary with its strong Norman tower and tall crooked spire. Until about 1926 the Hurst was entered by a narrow entry as a building known as the Armoury occupied most of the site. The building was used as the town's administrative centre. The building on the left with the cupola is the Oddfellows Hall, which was erected in 1891. In 1905 it was capable of holding 300 people and was used for public entertainment.

Opposite below: Cressage, *c.* 1930. This view is looking back down the main road towards Shrewsbury with the post office on the left and the Eagles public house on the right behind the second car. In 1930 the post office dealt with all the usual post that came via the Shrewsbury sorting office and also money orders, telegrams and telephone calls. In 1901 the Eagles was owned by Lord Barnard and occupied by George Holmes. The inn consisted of a bar, a parlour, a sitting room, a front room, seven bedrooms, cellars, brew house and stabling for four horses. Mr Holmes was considered a good landlord although on 18 June 1898 he was found guilty of 'harbouring a constable' and fined a pound, which included costs.

St Mary's Church, Cleobury Mortimer, *c.* 1920. The church stands in the middle of the town and is the dominant feature. Most of the building is Early English in style but its tower is Norman. Its tall wooden steeple, which is covered in oak shingle, is warped by its age and by the weather, giving it a quaint twisted look. The steeple was added in 1761 and has been painted white on several occasions. The Victorian east window was given to the church by the Revd Edward Baldwyn-Childe in 1875 and is a memorial to the poet William Langland, who was born in Cleobury Mortimer in 1332. His poem, 'Visions of Piers Ploughman' is one of the masterpieces of medieval English literature.

The High Street, Cleobury Mortimer, *c.* 1950. The timber-framed building is the Talbot, which was first licensed in about 1800. At the start of the twentieth century it belonged to the Bridgnorth Brewery. Its accommodation included an entrance hall, clubroom, bar, market room, sitting room, smoke room, nine bedrooms and stabling for nine horses. The timber façade is Victorian and was added in 1871 to mask a much older wooden structure. A cattle market was opened at the back of the hotel in April 1902 with room for 500 cattle, 1,000 sheep and 200 pigs. Note the mounting block in front of the hotel to help customers slightly the worse for drink to mount their horses. The bakery with the Hovis sign above the front door was also a café serving teas and refreshments.

The High Street, Cleobury Mortimer, 24 October 1962. Mrs Edith Harris, who had lived in the town for forty years, enjoying some late autumn sunshine. She is sitting by the stump of the old stone cross, said to mark the spot where Hugh de Mortimer erected a gallows in the thirteenth century and where the body of Prince Arthur was laid in 1502, on its journey from Ludlow to Worcester. The monumental horse trough and drinking fountain is a memorial to Captain Trow, who died of fever in South Africa during the Boer War.

The post office, Cleobury Mortimer, *c.* 1905. The Downes family ran the post office and general store for well over a hundred years. In 1851 there were two grocers in Cleobury called Downes, John in the High Street and Thomas in Lower Town. The postmaster at this time was William Jefferies. In 1872 Thomas Downes was listed as a grocer and miller and by 1885 Thomas Downes junior had become the postmaster. The Downes family flourished and the *Kelly's Directory* for 1905 confirms that Thomas was not only sub-postmaster but also a grocer and provisions merchant, an agent for Allsopp's brewery, a fire and life insurance agent and the owner of a watermill. This view shows the staff at the post office with possibly Mr Downes standing in the doorway. The town's most famous postman was Simon Evans, who wrote and broadcast about the area he worked in. He also wrote several books, the first in 1931 entitled *Round About The Crooked Steeple*.

The Eagle and Serpent, Kinlet, *c.* 1905. The unusual name of the inn is taken from the coat of arms of the Childe family who were the principal landowners in the area. The inn was owned in 1901 by Charlotte A. Childe who lived at Kinlet Hall. It was occupied by Mrs Elizabeth Humphreys who had taken the inn over from her husband William. On the ground floor there were a bar, parlour, sitting room, kitchen and a clubroom, while upstairs there were four bedrooms. A previous landlord, Edward Bytheway, was taken to court in July 1885 for 'allowing liquor to be consumed on his premises during prohibited hours'. He was fined 40*s* plus 10*s* 10*d* costs.

Ditton Priors, *c.* 1905. Ditton Priors is an isolated village situated at about 800ft on the side of Brown Clee. In the early years of the twentieth century the village was involved with the quarrying at the top of the Clee and a railway line was built between Cleobury Mortimer and Ditton Priors to move the stone that was much in demand for making roads. During the Second World War the navy commandeered the line to ferry arms when they opened a depot in the village. In 1967 the depot was taken over by the United States army who remained there for a number of years. Today the depot has been converted into an industrial estate.

Below: The post office and Well Farm, Farlow, *c.* 1925. Farlow lies at a crossroads in the shadow of the Brown Clee. The name of the village is derived from 'fern hill'. At the beginning of the twentieth century the village was fairly busy, having a church, Wesleyan chapel, school, shop, post office, blacksmith, carpenter, watermill and two inns, the Gate and the Plough. In 1917 the Plough Inn was tenanted by the Carloss family who later occupied Well Farm for many years. The village shop and post office was run by sub-postmaster David Price. Incoming mail was brought from Cleobury Mortimer while outgoing items could be posted at the post office or at two wall boxes near the school and the Gate Inn.

Clee Hill village, *c.* 1930. This view is looking down the A4117 towards Angel Bank and Ludlow. The Victoria Inn on the right was granted a full licence in 1868. At the time of the 1901 census the inn was owned by Richard Hatton who lived in Ludlow but leased it to the Ludlow and Craven Arms Brewery Company. The inn was managed by John Martin and consisted of a bar, parlour, taproom, clubroom, kitchen, three bedrooms and stabling for five horses. The census also reports that the house required painting and whitewashing throughout, the stables needed repairing and that there was no urinal. In July 1893 the landlord was taken to court for allowing drunkenness on his licenced premises and for permitting disorderly conduct in his house. He was fined 5s plus 8s costs for the first offence, but the second charge was withdrawn.

Rouse Broughton Terrace, Dhustone, *c.* 1930. The tiny hamlet of Dhustone stands on the side of Titterstone Clee just off the Ludlow to Kidderminster road. The settlement takes its name from the stone that was quarried from there, which was ideal for road making. The hard, dark igneous rock is called dhu stone, which is derived from the Celtic for black stone. The Victorian houses, built for the quarrymen, look out of place on the side of the rugged hillside. They are named after Sir Charles Henry Rouse-Broughton of Downton Hall who was listed as one of the principal landowners in the area. The single-storey building on the left is the village hall while at the bottom of the road is the bridge that takes traffic over the now disused mineral railway line.

7

AROUND LUDLOW, CRAVEN ARMS, CLUN & BISHOP'S CASTLE

Ludlow from the Whitcliffe, *c.* 1930. Dominating the skyline is the lofty tower of the parish church of St Laurence, which was described by the writer John Leland in the sixteenth century as 'very fayer and large, and richly adorned, and taken for the fayrest in all these quarters.' In the foreground are the gardens below Dinham and Camp Lane. The large white house to the left with the entrance porch and conservatory at the side is Dinham Lodge, which was built in about 1800. The building to the right with the white turret in the centre of the roof contains part of a chapel erected in the twelfth century and dedicated to St Thomas Becket.

Lower Broad Street, Ludlow, *c.* 1890. At the top of the street is the Broad Gate, the last of the five main gateways into town. This area of town was where the poorer people involved in the town's busy cloth industry lived. Note the magnificent sign of the Bell on the right, once one of the major coaching inns on the main southern road out of Ludlow. The building with the two dormer windows facing down the street is the Wheatsheaf, which was first recorded in 1753. Today this is a very pleasant area of Ludlow in which to live, the only problem being where to park your car! The Bell was closed around 1896 and is now a private residence called Old Bell House. The Wheatsheaf is still an inn and is the last survivor of nine public houses that once existed in this part of Ludlow. It is also reputed to be the last hostelry in the town to brew its own beer.

Broad Street, Ludlow, *c.* 1925. A small house fire occurred on the premises of the Fancy Warehouse occupied by Miss Sarah Frances Smith. The photograph was taken by Walter Harper, a local photographer whose studio was situated on the opposite side of the road. The lorry just below the building belonged to John Bowdler, a builder from Brand Lane. At the top of the street is the Butter Cross that was built by the Corporation in 1743. The main entrance is in the centre of the building through an open porch supported by four Tuscan pillars. It was designed by William Baker of Audlem in Cheshire and cost around £1,000.

The Butter Cross, Ludlow, *c.* 1950. This view of the Butter Cross is from the High Street looking towards King Street. The Butter Cross replaced an older timber-framed building that was erected in 1570 and was known as the New House. The open ground floor of the Cross was used for selling dairy products while the upper rooms have been used as a school room, a workingman's evening club and for civic functions. Over the years it has been described as a 'richly wrought little jewel,' and 'a great ornament to the town' by eminent visitors to Ludlow and it has always been a subject for artists and photographers to capture. The timber-framed building on the corner of King Street and Broad Street was erected at the beginning of the seventeenth century. Bodenhams moved their business there in 1900 from another shop in King Street, selling a full range of men and boys' wear.

Castle Square, Ludlow, *c.* 1950. The large building is the Town Hall, which was built in 1887 to commemorate the Golden Jubilee of Queen Victoria. It cost around £6,000 and was designed by Henry A. Cheers of Twickenham. In *Kelly's Directory* of 1891 it was described as 'a handsome building of red brick and Bath stone dressing in the Renaissance style.' Nearly a hundred years later, as fashions changed, it was described by Nikolaus Pevsner as 'Ludlow's bad luck,' and was demolished in March 1986. The building on the right is Castle Lodge, built in about 1564 for Thomas Sackford, an official for the Council of the Marches. The cannon was Russian and a gift to the town from the government in 1857.

Castle Street, Ludlow, *c.* 1900. The eastern end of Castle Street was known locally as Post Office Square from the post office at No. 6, run at this time by Postmaster William Price. On the left is the end of the old Town Hall and to the right is the end of The Rows. The building at the end of Church Street and Harp Lane housed the business of Fredrick Larcombe. In 1905 he was a cycle agent but also sold sewing machines, mangles, mail carts and musical instruments for cash or 'by easy payment system'.

Ludlow Castle, *c.* 1930. The castle was built by the Normans on this natural defensive site overlooking the River Teme. Until 1689 it was the headquarters of the Council of the Marches, which maintained law and order along the border between England and Wales for several hundred years. Compare the large open outer bailey to the cramped inner baily, which was entered through the massive square keep and protected by a deep ditch. To the left of the keep are the Judges' Lodgings and in the centre of the inner bailey is the unique rounded Norman nave of St Mary Magdalene Chapel. Overlooking the Teme are the living quarters, which included the Solar, Great Hall, Great Chamber and Tudor lodgings.

Milton's *Masque of Comus*, Ludlow Castle, July 1934. This epic restaging of Milton's classic marked the 300th anniversary of its premier, performed to mark the first visit of the Lord President of The Marches, the Earl of Bridgwater. The play was performed again in 1953, 1958 and 1959 as a fundraising exercise for St Laurence's Church. Its success led to the foundation of the first Ludlow Festival in 1960. This is a scene from Episode Three, the Trial of Prince David of Wales at Shrewsbury, 30 September 1283. Acting in this scene are Lady Berwick, Lady Anne Bridgeman and Lady Joan Bridgeman.

Bromfield post office, *c.* 1910. At the beginning of the twentieth century William Wadeley was sub-postmaster and to supplement his wage he was also the village tailor. Incoming mail reached the post office at 4.30 a.m. and outgoing mail left at 6 a.m. and 8.30 p.m. There is a meadow in Bromfield called The Crawls, which was once the site of a moated mansion. The owner had a beautiful daughter who fell in love with a penniless knight. This so angered the father that he swore the only dowry she would receive would be the land she could crawl around on a harsh winter's night. Wearing leather breeches, she amazed her father by crawling all the way to Downton. He was so impressed he made her his heiress over her brothers.

Ashford Carbonell, *c*. 1900. The name Ashford is derived from the ford and the great ash that stood by it; they are thought to have been situated a little further downstream than the present bridge. Carbonell was the family name of the lord of the manor, William Carbonell. The houses all straggle along the main street and are a mixture of architectural styles. The funeral cortège of Prince Arthur, eldest son of Henry VII, is believed to have used this route on its way back to London.

The Salwey Arms, Wooferton, *c*. 1970. The inn has been fully licensed since 1853. In 1900 the owner was Mrs O'Brian of Moor Park, Ludlow, and the landlady was Elizabeth Gittins. This photograph was taken when it was discovered that the licensee, Mr Harold Moulton, and his sister Phyllis had been bound and gagged after a midnight raid. Mr Moulton was Shropshire's longest serving landlord at the time. The robbers got away with over £200.

Market Street, Craven Arms, *c.* 1950. The shops on the right belonged to the Miller family. The ladies are standing outside the premises of Walter Miller, who was originally a house furnisher but later changed to selling bicycles. The grocery shop was run by Mrs Martha Miller, who moved there at the beginning of the twentieth century after establishing her business around the corner in Dale Street in 1898. The house with the army recruiting sign over the front door is Bristol House on the corner of Dale Street. At the end of the nineteenth century it was the post office run by Edwin Thomas, who was also a local corn merchant. The house was later used as offices for auctioneer, valuer and estate agent Charles Edwards, before becoming Mrs Edwards' Refreshment Rooms. The notice inside the door announces the sale of teas, luncheons and snacks.

Market Street, Craven Arms, *c.* 1920. This is the Clun Valley Motor Service Omnibus at the Ludlow end of Market Street. It served villages in the south of Shropshire and was driven by Harry Wood, known locally as 'Conk' due to his large nose and the bus was known as 'Conk's Henhouse'. It is parked outside the Shropshire Motor Garage, which was managed by A.E. Bowen. The garage was an authorised Ford Service Depot and was also able to supply and mend aircraft. At the bottom of the road is the Stokesay Castle Hotel & Posting House, which also had a garage and inspection pit.

Newton, Craven Arms, *c.* 1900. Newton was a small settlement on the eastern side of the A49. In the middle of the nineteenth century the settlement was absorbed into the new town of Craven Arms. The building on the right is a section of the Lion or Red Lion Inn that had been in operation since at least 1768. Around 1898 the licence was transferred to the newly opened Stokesay Hotel and the old inn was demolished in the 1920s. The timber-framed house opposite still stands with its massive chimney stack, which is thought to be part of a tower used as a lookout post during the Civil War. The building below is the premises of Thomas Griffith a carpenter and wheelwright, who, according to the sign on the side of the building, was also the local painter and decorator.

Newton Street, Craven Arms, *c.* 1910. Stokesay Castle Hotel is on the right with Stokesay School at the rear. The first national school was built near the church at Stokesay in 1858 and was enlarged in 1886 to accommodate 162 children. With the rapid growth of the town and a series of critical reports by inspectors, it was decided to build a new school near the centre of town. It opened on 31 August 1896 and cost between £2,000 and £3,000. The headmaster, Mr Thomas Mountford, transferred with the children and remained in the post until he retired in 1925.

Market day, Clun, *c.* 1900. The excited children are standing outside the post office, run for many years by Jessie Cooke. Top left is the sign of the Buffalo Hotel and below is the wagon belonging to Rix's grocery store in the High Street. The white building in the centre is the North and South Wales Bank, which only opened on Tuesdays from 11 a.m. until 2 p.m. and on fair days; they were backed by the London Westminster Bank. Sherwood's butcher's shop is on the corner of the buildings on the right and next to them is the White Horse Inn, run for many years by Mrs Graves, who died in the early 1920s aged eighty-five. The wheel in front of the inn was used to wind drinking water up from the well. A poultry dealer sits on his crates of chickens, while a 'cricker', the local name for a travelling china salesman, sets out his wares on the pavement.

High Street, Clun, *c.* 1930. The large house on the right is Creswell House in Bridge Street. The shop next door was a draper and outfitter run by T. and A. Hamar; the premises are now converted into two cottages known as Albany House and Alpha Cottage. On the left is the Malt House, built in 1619. By 1819 Richard Thomas was the maltster, but by 1841 the business had been taken over by George Hamar. At the beginning of the twentieth century it was an inn called the Old Talbot, run by Joe Luther.

The Bell Procession, Clun, 22 July 1914. The bells had been recast in London and were returned by rail to Broome station. There they were met by two decorated drays, local clergymen, church officials, almsmen and a horde of excited children. They were then paraded back to Clun for the welcoming home of the bells ceremony. Here the parade is seen marching down Church Street, carrying banners with the legends 'God Bless The Bells', 'Pease Bee Unto Clun 1668', and 'Welcome The Bells'. Hymns were sung by the lychgate, and after an address from the vicar everyone paraded round to the vicarage for a refreshing tea and sports events. The building by the bridge is the Temperance Hall, erected in 1870, now converted into the Bridge Crafts and Coffee Shop.

Almsmen, Clun, 9 September 1935. Four members of Holy Trinity Hospital stand by the lychgate outside St George's Church, dressed in their traditional uniform. This consisted of a hat and a dark blue coat with the coat-of-arms of the founder, a rampant silver lion on a red background. The formidable character in the centre is John Weale of Newcastle-on-Clun. He was known as 'Joe the Bear', a nickname he earned by wrestling bears at the May Fair in Knighton. In later life he contented himself by sitting on a bench in the middle of Clun and tripping up girls and young ladies with his walking stick. There is a statue commemorating 'Joe the Bear' at the hospital. The two almsmen on the right are Mr Whittle and Mr Edwards.

Bishop's Castle from the church tower, *c.* 1930. Bishop's Castle was described by Sir Richard Colt Hoare in his diary in June 1799 in this way: 'I found a comfortable inn (the Castle). The Inn, its garden and the bowling green above it occupy the space of the Bishop's castle – here the bishop formerly resided-til about the time of Q. Elizabeth. The town is a borough – commanded by Lord Clive – dreary and dull – the ground around it is uncommonly rich and valuable – owing probably to the quantity of manure running down on it from the town on all sides. (Inn Good).'

The House on Crutches, Bishop's Castle, 2 April 1986. The house takes its name from the supports under the upper storey. In 1986 the Old Castle Land Trust purchased the house and an appeal was launched for its restoration, which was sympathetically carried out by 1988. During the restoration a number of modern carvings were added. It is now a museum covering different areas of local life and is run by volunteers at weekends.

Market Square, Bishop's Castle, *c.* 1900. The building in the centre is the old Market Hall. It was built in the second half of the eighteenth century and was later used as a reading room and was known as the Powis Institute. There were seventy members in 1905 and for a fee they were able to peruse a supply of daily newspapers and periodicals. The local lodge of Oddfellows also met in one of the rooms there. The building was demolished in 1951 but the Powis coat-of-arms over the top window has been preserved in the Square. The arms contain a figure of an elephant to commemorate Lord Clive's achievements in India. The agricultural implements in front of the hall belong to Arthur Greenhous, a local ironmonger, whose shop was just to the right.

The Three Tuns, Salop Street, Bishop's Castle, *c.* 1910. Nearly thirty public houses have been identified in Bishop's Castle, but the most famous is the Three Tuns. It was bought quite by chance by John Roberts, a tea taster from London, in 1888 and it was run by the Roberts family for three generations until his grandson, also called John, retired in 1976. The first thing Mr Roberts did after buying the inn was build a new brewery. He also employed his cousin, who was teetotal, to brew the beer! Brewing is still carried out there today and the beer is always of the highest standard.

Bishop's Castle railway station, *c.* 1905. The first section of the railway was opened on 1 February 1866 and it was hoped that the line would travel on to Montgomery and from there to the Welsh coast. The railway, which left the main line just above Craven Arms, covered around 18 miles and had stations at Horderley, Plowden, Eaton, Lydham Heath and Bishop's Castle. The platform and the main station buildings are on the right with the carriage shed just to the left of the signal. The men are posing with an engine that was built in Wolverhampton in 1869 and was bought by the Bishop's Castle Railway in 1905.

The Arbour Tree, Aston-on-Clun, *c.* 1925. This English or native poplar tree stood on that site for about 300 years until it was blown over during a heavy gale in 1995. During a ceremony held each year on Oak Apple Day, 29 May, the tree is decorated with flags hung on long larch poles. According to local tradition the flags commemorate the wedding of John Marston of Aston-on-Clun and Mary Carter of Sibdon, who were married on that day in 1786. Historians believe that the tradition is much older and dates back to Celtic times when women's clothing was hung on special trees during the planting season to ensure the fertility of the soil. A new poplar has been planted in the village and the tree dressing ceremony is still performed each year.

Bucknell forge, *c*. 1900. Bucknell has always been a thriving little village. As well as the usual amenities there were also a thatcher, a cobbler, a coal merchant, a steam threshing machine proprietor, a wheelwright, a blacksmith and four public houses. At the end of the nineteenth century the smithy and one of the public houses, the Plough Inn, were run by the same man, John Dodd. In 1885 he advertised: 'One minute's walk from the Station, a good horse and trap for hire, good stabling, well-aired beds'.

Stokesay Castle, *c*. 1920. The de Say family were the Norman tenants of the manor, and shortly after 1068 Picot de Say built a castle and church on this site. Lawrence de Ludlow, a wealthy wool merchant, built the fortified manor house in about 1280. During the Civil War the church of St John the Baptist on the left was badly damaged by the Roundheads and was restored between 1654 and 1664, resulting in a rare Commonwealth church.

8

AROUND STRETTON VALE

All Stretton, *c.* 1930. The village lies north-east of Church Stretton, between the Long Mynd on the west and Caer Caradoc to the east. Stretton is derived from 'Street Town', but according to local folklore King Charles II named the three settlements. Arriving at Little Stretton the King enquired his whereabouts, 'At Stretton if you please', replied a countryman. 'Little Stretton is a fitter name for so small a place', said the King and rode on towards Shrewsbury. On reaching the next village he again asked where he was. 'At Stretton', someone answered. Seeing the parish church whose bells were ringing in the old grey steeple, His Majesty exclaimed, 'call it Church Stretton', and went on his way once more. Finally the King approached the next village and was again informed he was at Stretton. 'Stretton!' cried Charles in astonishment, 'why it's all Stretton about here!'

The Manor House, All Stretton, *c.* 1900. Part of the timber-framed building dates from about 1600. For a time in the early nineteenth century it became a maltings, but was later used as a lodging house for tramps and was licensed to sleep thirteen men, who had to spend the night standing up with their arms over a rope strung across the room. They were woken in the morning by the owner, who untied one end of the rope. No food was supplied, but any traveller who brought his own was allowed to warm it over the open fire. On the wall hung the following rules: 'No drink allowed on the premises. No bad language to be used. No drums to be used here. No washing on Saturday or Sunday. No smoking upstairs. Couples to wash their own pots.' At the beginning of the twentieth century the house was restored and was called the Manor House for the first time.

Cwm Spring Mineral Waters, All Stretton, *c.* 1910. The Stretton Hills Mineral Water Co. opened a factory on the Shrewsbury Road in 1883. It became one of the area's main employers and was known locally as the 'Pop Works'. Jewsbury & Brown ran it for many years until it was taken over by Wells' Drinks of Tenbury Wells. At the beginning of the twentieth century Francis Sutton FCS, FIC wrote, 'This is one of the purest waters which has ever come to my notice.' Dr W.D. Thursfield, the Medical Officer of Health for Shropshire, wrote, 'For gouty people the water of Cwm Dale is especially suited.'

Sandford Avenue, Church Stretton, *c.* 1910. The avenue takes its name from the Revd Holland Sandford, rector of Eaton-under-Haywood. It was formerly known as Station Road and is the principal shopping area of the town. The shop with the clock over the door was one of the first plots to be developed on this road. It was occupied by Thomas Rich, a watchmaker and cycle dealer. He was responsible for the clock but after he left it fell into disrepair. It was restored with the aid of the town's Civic Society some years later.

High Street, Church Stretton, *c.* 1900. The monument on the right was a drinking fountain erected to commemorate Queen Victoria's Diamond Jubilee in 1897. It was moved just a few years later to a site in front of Burway House where it remained until 1963, when it was taken down after a large vehicle had hit it, displacing the upper half. The plinth was demolished but the top section was 'stored', under a hedge in the town's cemetery, where it was later discovered. The buildings on both corners of the road have also been demolished.

High Street, Church Stretton, *c.* 1945. With the rapid growth of the town at the beginning of the twentieth century banks were keen to get established in the town. On the left is Lloyds Bank and on the right is the Midland Bank, built on the site once occupied by the drinking fountain. Both banks were erected in the early 1920s. Note the white telephone box by Lloyds Bank.

High Street, Church Stretton, *c.* 1905. This is a view of the Town Hall and market, looking south. The traders sold their wares beneath the arches, while the business of the town was conducted in the room above. The upper storey was also used for concerts and public meetings and had a capacity of around 250. In 1869 fortnightly penny readings took place there for the benefit of the working classes. It was a square building of red brick with a stone dressing, supported on stone pillars. A contemporary account considered the building as 'neither beautiful to the eye or with any pretensions to architectural excellence'. It was demolished in 1958 after it was found to be unsafe.

Opposite: The Hotel, Church Stretton, *c.* 1910. Stretton's most central hotel was built in three phases on the site of a farmhouse, an inn and a malt house. The first phase on the corner in 1861 replaced the Crown Inn and malt house. The second phase on Sandford Avenue was built in 1899, and the final phase along the Shrewsbury Road on the site of the farmhouse was completed in 1906. An inscribed stone from the old malt house has been retained. It reads, 'Erected by Copper A W his sonne Ano Dni 1587.'

St Lawrence's church, Church Stretton, *c*. 1930. Parts of the church date back to Norman times. The tower is late fifteenth to early sixteenth century and contains eight bells, six cast by Abraham Rudhall in 1711 and two more added later. The chiming clock was a gift from the rector, the Revd C. Noel Hill, in 1890. This message to bell ringers was placed in the belfry in 1773: 'If you ring and do come here, You must ring well with hand and ear, And if the bell you overthrow, 4*d* to pay before you go, And if you ring in spur or hat, 6*d* you must pay for that, or in this place you swear and curse, 12*d* to pay pull out your purse.'

Cardingmill Valley, 22 May 1961. This valley has attracted visitors for many years, especially in the late 1950s and early '60s. At weekends hundreds of visitors from all over Shropshire and the Midlands would descend upon the valley for a pleasant day out. For the active there were walks up to the Light Spout Waterfall, to Mott's Road or to the ancient Bodbury Ring. For the less energetic a quiet picnic by the stream or an ice cream and a cup of tea at the Chalet Pavilion were pleasant ways to spend an afternoon.

The Chalet Pavilion, Cardingmill Valley, *c.* 1930. The pavilion was made in sections and imported from Scandinavia. It closed during the Second World War but reopened in 1947, when they advertised that 'Every type of meal is supplied. Morning coffee, hot and cold lunches, meat teas or just a pot of tea and cake. Seats 250 and is a favourite rendezvous for works outings, social and sports clubs and Sunday school parties.' The National Trust bought the pavilion in 1978 and the tradition of warm hospitality to walkers and ramblers has continued.

The Ragleth Inn, Little Stretton, *c.* 1935. In 1900 there were three inns in the village, the Green Dragon, the Sun and the Crown. The Crown closed and was converted into the village shop. The Green Dragon is still in existence but the Sun has changed its name to the Ragleth, commemorating the hill near by. The sign outside the inn reads, 'Luncheons, Teas, Board Residence'. The cottages on the left are still called The Ancient House.

All Saints' Church, Little Stretton, *c.* 1920. This church was erected and paid for by Mrs Gibbon from the Manor House and was opened on 20 October 1903. It is an iron structure, ornamented in wood to give it a timber-framed appearance. It was bought from a firm in Manchester specialising in this type of building and was assembled by local workmen. A thatched roof was added in 1935, paid for by Derwent Wood from the Old Tan House, and gives it a more rustic appearance.

Leebotwood, *c.* 1900. The name of the village originates from the clearing in the forest of Botwood. The photographer is looking south towards Church Stretton and Ludlow. The Pound Inn on the left was occupied at this time by Thomas Hotchkiss Everson and owned by the Revd F.H.W. Whitmore of Dudmaston, who sold it to the People's Refreshment House Association around 1914. In the 1901 census of public houses the inn consisted of a bar, a parlour, a private room, a kitchen, three cellars and four bedrooms. The house also contains some fine oak panelling, which is thought to originate from Woolstaston Rectory. The inn takes its name from the enclosure used by drovers to impound their cattle while spending the night in the inn.

Cardington, August 1961. Cardington is an attractive little village, built mainly of stone, 3½ miles north-east of Church Stretton. Behind the Royal Oak is the church of St James. The nave is Norman and up to 800 years old, while the tower is a mixture of early English and perpendicular styles. Inside is a handsome memorial to Judge William Leighton, the Chief Justice, who lived nearby at Plaish Hall. He died in 1607.

Rushbury station, *c.* 1910. The station was on the Great Western Railway line that formed a direct route from Wellington to Craven Arms, via Much Wenlock. The line also had stops at Buildwas, Presthope and Longville. Passenger and freight services stopped in the 1950s and the line was lifted. The old station was then converted into a private house.

Miss Fanny Jones' Tea Place, Chelmick, 21 September 1954. The tearoom at Chelmick near Hope Bowdler was a Mecca for hikers and walkers in the Stretton Hills. Miss Jones, shown here, ran the tea room with her sisters Sarah and Mary Ellen. The café opened just before the First World War and was in operation until 1955, when a fire burnt down the cottage. Visitors still remember the wonderful teas spread before them, with up to twenty-four varieties of home-made cake. The beautiful wisteria is thought to have been grown from a cutting from a tree at the Boathouse in Shrewsbury. It survived the fire and grew up the building that replaced the cottage.

9

PEACEFUL VILLAGES & HAMLETS

Acton Burnell, *c.* 1950. This view is looking towards the crossroads from the Longnor road. The people on the left watching the photographer are opposite the village school. At one time there were two schools in the village, the Public Elementary School – on this view – and the Catholic School. The elementary school was built in 1815 to accommodate sixty children and was enlarged in 1901 to accommodate ninety, while the Catholic school was built in 1877 for sixty pupils. In 1905 the average weekly attendance at the elementary school was eighty-four, while at the Catholic school it was just thirteen.

Bridge Farm, Buildwas, *c.* 1930. The photographer is standing on the road bridge that carries traffic from Buildwas to Cressage. He is looking downstream to Ironbridge. The bridge over the Severn at this point gives the farm its name. The original structure was built out of stone but it was damaged during the Great Flood of 1795. It was replaced the following year by an iron structure designed by Thomas Telford at a cost of £6,444. At the beginning of the twentieth century Telford's bridge had become unsafe owing to earth movement on both banks and was replaced by a girder bridge made by the Horsehay Company in 1905. At one time the picturesque farm building was an inn called the Abbey Hotel, taking its name from the Cistercian monastery just across the bridge.

The Bell Inn, Cross Houses, c. 1905. A boy cleaning up the yard poses for the photographer by the water pump. From the 1890s until the early 1920s the inn was run by Francis Yates and then by his wife Mary. In 1901 it was owned by Soames' Brewery of Wrexham and contained a parlour, a smoke-room, a bar, a taproom, a kitchen, eight bedrooms and a cellar. There was a stable for four horses and the whole premises were clean and in a good state of repair. In November 1893 Mr Yates was taken to court for allowing drunkenness on licensed premises. He was fined £3 plus 10s costs and had his licence endorsed; a much greater punishment than the landlord of the Cound Lodge Inn who committed a similar offence. Within a few years of the photograph being taken the whole frontage was altered quite considerably.

Cound Lodge Inn, Cound, *c*. 1905. The driver of the pony and trap enjoys a read and a pipe of tobacco while waiting for a fare. This side of the inn was originally the back of the building until the middle of the nineteenth century. The main road once ran between the inn and the river but was diverted to the rear to make way for the Severn Valley railway line. In 1901 the owner was James Thursby-Pelham who lived at Harnage House, Dorrington. The landlord was William Milner and the inn consisted of two kitchens, two parlours, a tap-room, ten bedrooms, a brew-house and a cellar. In June 1890 and again in March 1898 the landlord was convicted of permitting drunkenness on his licensed premises. On the last occasion he was fined 10*s* 6*d* plus 16*s* 6*d* costs. In 1905 the landlord was John G. Jones who was also listed as a farmer. He advertised that teas were provided for cyclists, tourists and pleasure parties and that boats could be hired from the inn.

Highley, *c*. 1900. The sinking of the pit and the influx of miners and their families brought a great deal of prosperity to the area and a number of shops opened in the village. One of the largest was the store in the centre belonging to James Frederick Lloyd, who was listed as a grocer, baker, stationer, general merchant, clothier and boot and shoe warehouseman. He was also the sub-postmaster with mail arriving there each morning from Bridgnorth at 7.55. Mr Lloyd's greatest competition came from a shop run by the Kidderminster Co-operative Society and a number of small establishments. Although most of the inhabitants of the village were linked with the mine, a rural life still flourished in the area, with a number of farmers being listed in the village along with associated tradesmen such as a blacksmith, a wheelwright and a miller.

Kinnerley, *c.* 1925. The red sandstone church is dedicated to St Mary and consists of a Perpendicular tower and a Georgian nave and chancel designed by James Farnolls Pritchard and built between 1773 and 1774. The tower was restored in 1862, in memory of Lilla Frances, who had died the previous year and was the wife of the vicar, the Revd E.W.O. Bridgeman. Another Bridgeman is buried in the churchyard. He is the Right Revd John Bridgeman who was Bishop of Chester from 1619 until his death at Morton Hall in 1652. The Bishop was also one of King James II's chaplains. The building at the end of the road is the National School.

The Nesscliffe Hotel, Nesscliffe, *c.* 1910. The hotel stands on what used to be the busy London to Holyhead road. The hotel was granted a six-day license in about 1800. In 1896 it was owned by Henry Hearne, who ran the Circus Brewery by the Welsh Bridge in Shrewsbury. The landlady was Emma Dodd, who kept the building in good repair but it was reported that the rooms were in need of cleaning. In 1895, she was found guilty of selling adulterated gin and fined 10*s* plus costs.

Maesbury Marsh, *c.* 1930. The village lies about 3 miles south of Oswestry on the Shropshire Union Canal. During the first half of the nineteenth century, the settlement developed into a port with a wharf, warehouses, grain store, and flour mill and bone-glue factory. The Navigation Inn on the right is a reminder of those days when narrow boats were hauled along the canal by horses. In the 1896 census, the inn was owned by the Ellesmere Brewery. The landlord was Frederick Hyde who ran the inn until about 1925, when it was taken over by his wife Emma. The inn had ten rooms and stables for seven horses. During the 1850s, the landlord was taken to court on several occasions for staying open outside licensed hours and for allowing drunkenness on his licensed premises.

Woolston, *c.* 1920. St Winifred's Well lies 1½ miles south-west of West Felton. It is believed that the body of this seventh-century saint was rested there. While being transported to Shrewsbury Abbey in 1138, where the body was rested, a miraculous spring bubbled up. The waters are supposed to have special powers and said to be good for treating cuts, bruises and even broken bones. The timber-framed building dates from about 1600 and until 1824 was the courthouse of the manor. By the end of the nineteenth century it had been converted into a dwelling. By the early eighteenth century the well attracted quite a number of visitors and between May and September several booths were set up to sell food and ale. Behaviour declined and the frolics were banned in about 1755.

Ruyton-XI-Towns, *c.* 1905. The photographer has his back to the road to Shottatton, looking towards the road to Baschurch. Another road to the left leads to Wykey. The cross was erected on the site of the village lock-up and was unveiled in April 1881, some thirty years after it had been first suggested. It was the work of Richard Dodson, a monumental mason from Swan Hill in Shrewsbury and it was paid for by Miss Orde, the sister-in-law of the vicar, the Revd Frederick Wilkinson. The cross was supposed to incorporate a drinking fountain but this never materialised and there were many complaints from villagers that the light in the alcove beneath the cross was often never lit.

Baschurch, *c.* 1905. Baschurch is a large village with quite a number of shops to cater for the community's needs. At the beginning of the twentieth century there were two boot-makers, a basket-maker, a tailor, three coal agents, a blacksmith, a painter and decorator, three grocery and provision shops, a butcher and three public houses. This corner shop was also the bakery and belonged to Fox-Davies and Passmore. They were also corn dealers and from their windows and adverts also sold wool, drapery and boots.

Harmer Hill, *c.* 1925. The children are standing next to the village pump. Note the machinery in front, which was presumably used to draw the water up from a deep well to feed the pump. The large building in the background is the Red Castle Inn. It was owned in 1896 by John Price Lee, who lived in Harmer Hill, but was run by Abraham Aldred, who in earlier directories was listed as a beer retailer. The house was said to be clean and in good repair but the stables needed a great deal of work. The general store, with its adverts for Cadbury and Bournville Cocoa, was owned by Percy Samuel Dove who traded there from the mid-1920s to the early 1930s.

Bomere Heath, *c.* 1905. The village was described in *Kelly's Directory* in 1905 as: 'a scattered village, partly in the parishes of St Alkmund's, Shrewsbury, Fitz and Preston Gubbals or Gobalds, and is adjunct to the ecclesiastical parish of Leaton 4¾ miles north of Shrewsbury, 2 miles north-east from Fitz parish and half a mile north of Leaton railway station. Some years ago, this village was a large piece of open common land, with a sheet of water in the centre in the form of a bow, from which the name Bomere Heath is derived.' The first building on the left is the Red Lion Inn.

Cockshutt, *c.* 1920. This view is looking towards Ellesmere and the church, dedicated to St Simon and St Jude. The building on the left is the Red Lion, built as a coaching inn on the Shrewsbury to Chester road. It was owned by Earl Brownlow in the nineteenth century and, for a short time between 1891 and 1893, it was renamed the Brownlow Arms. The Dickin family ran the inn for many years and was responsible for renovating it. They also used some of the outbuildings as a slaughter house and a butcher's shop. In 1999, the name of the inn was changed to the Terra Nova and four years later to the Leaking Tap.

Ford, *c.* 1930. Two little boys pose for the photographer on the parapet of the bridge, which replaced the ford that gave the village its name. Behind the trees on the right is the church dedicated to St Michael. The church dates from the early thirteenth century but very little of the original structure survives, as it was heavily restored and enlarged in 1875 at a cost of £1,400. The cross in the centre of the new graveyard was erected in memory of the men who died in the First World War. It was paid for by public subscription and unveiled in 1920. The large building opposite the church is Mansion House, which dates from 1779. It has a three-bay pediment, with Louis XVI garlands. In 1929 it was the home of George William Jones, who was listed as a farmer.

Prees, *c.* 1910. The children on the left are standing outside a grocery shop advertising Anchor Tea, while the shop on the right has a large array of crockery in the window and are advertised as agents for Berries Dye Works. Further down on the right is the sign of the New Inn, the last of the twelve that catered for the coaching trade. In 1875 the landlord was fined £1 and had his licence endorsed for supplying spirits to a boy under sixteen. In 1896 the inn belonged to Thomas Adams of Edgmond and was occupied by Sarah Dutton who kept the house clean and in good repair.

Prees Heath, *c.* 1930. This fashionable outdoor swimming pool was very popular with swimmers and sun-worshippers from a wide area during the summer months. Note the fine statue, ornamental fountain, the slide, diving platform and springboard in the 7ft 6in deep end of the pool. The pool was situated at the rear of the Witch Ball Hotel and was there until the 1960s.

Hodnet, *c.* 1950. This is the main road through the village travelling from Market Drayton to Shrewsbury. The turn to Whitchurch on the A442 is on the right. The building on the left with the fine inn sign and the board on the pavement advertising lunch, tea and dinner is the Bear Inn. The Morris Minor is parked outside the shop belonging to William France, a tailor, and just beyond is the shop belonging to E. Taylor, which was later known as the Supply Stores when it was run by W.G. & F.M. Bennett.